D0200786

MAY 0 9 2011

DISCARD

Mental Health

Other Books in the Issues on Trial Series:

Mental Health

Sylvia Engdahl, Book Editor

GREENHAVEN PRESS
A part of Gale, Cengage Learning

Detroit • New York • San Francisco • New Haven, Conn • Waterville, Maine • London

GALE
CENGAGE Learning™

Christine Nasso, *Publisher*
Elizabeth Des Chenes, *Managing Editor*

© 2010 Greenhaven Press, a part of Gale, Cengage Learning

For more information, contact:
Greenhaven Press
27500 Drake Rd.
Farmington Hills, MI 48331-3535
Or you can visit our Internet site at gale.cengage.com.

ALL RIGHTS RESERVED
No part of this work covered by the copyright herein may be reproduced, transmitted, stored, or used in any form or by any means graphic, electronic, or mechanical, including but not limited to photocopying, recording, scanning, digitizing, taping, Web distribution, information networks, or information storage retrieval systems, except as permitted under Section 107 or 108 of the 1976 United States Copyright Act, without the prior written permission of the publisher.

For product information and technology assistance, contact us at

Gale Customer Support, 1-800-877-4253
For permission to use material from this text or product, submit all requests online at
www.cengage.com/permissions

Further permissions questions can be emailed to permissionrequest@cengage.com

Articles in Greenhaven Press anthologies are often edited for length to meet page requirements. In addition, original titles of these works are changed to clearly present the main thesis and to explicitly indicate the author's opinion. Every effort is made to ensure that Greenhaven Press accurately reflects the original intent of the authors. Every effort has been made to trace the owners of copyrighted material.

Cover photograph Mandel Ngan/AFP/Getty Images.

LIBRARY OF CONGRESS CATALOGING-IN-PUBLICATION DATA

Mental health / Sylvia Engdahl, book editor.
    p. cm. -- (Issues on trial)
    Includes bibliographical references and index.
    ISBN 978-0-7377-4738-6 (hbk.)
    1. Mental health--United States--Juvenile literature. 2. Mental illness--United States--Juvenile literature. 3. Mentally ill--Treatment--United States--Juvenile literature. I. Engdahl, Sylvia.
    RA790.6.M366 2010
    362.196'89--dc22
                                                                        2009043384

Printed in the United States of America
2 3 4 5 6 7 14 13 12 11 10

Contents

Chapter 3: Defining the Rights of Institutionalized Patients

Chapter 4: The Right to Live and Receive Treatment in the Community

The Supreme Court ruled that under the Americans with Disabilities Act (ADA), the states are required to provide community-based treatment for persons with mental disabilities when treatment professionals determine that such placement is appropriate, the affected persons do not oppose such treatment, and the placement can be reasonably accommodated.

Foreword

The U.S. courts have long served as a battleground for the most highly charged and contentious issues of the time. Divisive matters are often brought into the legal system by activists who feel strongly for their cause and demand an official resolution. Indeed, subjects that give rise to intense emotions or involve closely held religious or moral beliefs lay at the heart of the most polemical court rulings in history. One such case was *Brown v. Board of Education* (1954), which ended racial segregation in schools. Prior to *Brown*, the courts had held that blacks could be forced to use separate facilities as long as these facilities were equal to that of whites.

For years many groups had opposed segregation based on religious, moral, and legal grounds. Educators produced heartfelt testimony that segregated schooling greatly disadvantaged black children. They noted that in comparison to whites, blacks received a substandard education in deplorable conditions. Religious leaders such as Martin Luther King Jr. preached that the harsh treatment of blacks was immoral and unjust. Many involved in civil rights law, such as Thurgood Marshall, called for equal protection of all people under the law, as their study of the Constitution had indicated that segregation was illegal and un-American. Whatever their motivation for ending the practice, and despite the threats they received from segregationists, these ardent activists remained unwavering in their cause.

Those fighting against the integration of schools were mainly white southerners who did not believe that whites and blacks should intermingle. Blacks were subordinate to whites, they maintained, and society had to resist any attempt to break down strict color lines. Some white southerners charged that segregated schooling was *not* hindering blacks' education. For example, Virginia attorney general J. Lindsay Almond asserted, "With the help and the sympathy and the love and respect of the white people of the South, the colored man has risen under that educational process to a place of eminence and respect throughout the nation. It has served him well." So when the Supreme Court ruled against the segregationists in *Brown*, the South responded with vociferous cries of protest. Even government leaders criticized the decision. The governor of Arkansas, Orval Faubus, stated that he would not "be a party to any attempt to force acceptance of change to which the people are so overwhelmingly opposed." Indeed, resistance to integration was so great that when black students arrived at the formerly all-white Central High School in Arkansas, federal troops had to be dispatched to quell a threatening mob of protesters.

Nevertheless, the *Brown* decision was enforced and the South integrated its schools. In this instance, the Court, while not settling the issue to everyone's satisfaction, functioned as an instrument of progress by forcing a major social change. Historian David Halberstam observes that the *Brown* ruling "deprived segregationist practices of their moral legitimacy. . . . It was therefore perhaps the single most important moment of the decade, the moment that separated the old order from the new and helped create the tumultuous era just arriving." Considered one of the most important victories for civil rights, *Brown* paved the way for challenges to racial segregation in many areas, including on public buses and in restaurants.

In examining *Brown*, it becomes apparent that the courts play an influential role—and face an arduous challenge—in shaping the debate over emotionally charged social issues. Judges must balance competing interests, keeping in mind the high stakes and intense emotions on both sides. As exemplified by *Brown*, judicial decisions often upset the status quo and initiate significant changes in society. Greenhaven Press's Issues on Trial series captures the controversy surrounding influential court rulings and explores the social ramifications of such decisions from varying perspectives. Each anthology highlights one social issue—such as the death penalty, students' rights, or wartime civil liberties. Each volume then focuses on key historical and contemporary court cases that helped mold the issue as we know it today. The books include a compendium of primary sources—court rulings, dissents, and immediate reactions to the rulings—as well as secondary sources from experts in the field, people involved in the cases, legal analysts, and other commentators opining on the implications and legacy of the chosen cases. An annotated table of contents, an in-depth introduction, and prefaces that overview each case all provide context as readers delve into the topic at hand. To help students fully probe the subject, each volume contains book and periodical bibliographies, a comprehensive index, and a list of organizations to contact. With these features, the Issues on Trial series offers a well-rounded perspective on the courts' role in framing society's thorniest, most impassioned debates.

Introduction

The question of how to treat people who are mentally ill is highly controversial. In past eras people with mental illnesses were confined to "insane asylums," where they lived in conditions of degradation, physical abuse, and squalor. Mental health professionals now agree that such treatment was barbaric and that patients should receive supportive care. Opinions differ sharply, however, on what kind of treatment best serves their interests.

Most psychiatrists believe that people diagnosed with a mental illness can benefit from medical treatment even if they do not choose it willingly. The theory dominant in psychiatry today holds that mental illness is caused by a chemical imbalance in the brain that can be treated with medication. Many psychiatric drugs have unpleasant side effects, however, and they can cause permanent and sometimes harmful physical changes. Advocates of this type of treatment maintain that these effects are the lesser evil if the medication helps patients to think and behave more normally. When seriously ill patients refuse to take the medications, as they often do, some doctors feel that the drugs should be administered by force. These doctors argue that people resist medication only because they are too unwell to make sound judgments.

A minority of psychiatrists, along with concerned citizens and many former patients, strongly oppose the theory that psychiatric drugs are beneficial. They contend that there is no scientific evidence that chemical imbalances cause mental illness, and they believe that the drugs themselves damage the brain. These challengers to mainstream psychiatry maintain that although such drugs do make disturbed people more manageable, forcing medication on unwilling patients is unjustifiable, unless there is no other way to subdue someone who is dangerous to others. Arguing that the pharmaceutical companies promote psychiatric drugs for profit, this faction also holds that society supports medicating the mentally ill as a matter of convenience—that is, in order to avoid having to deal with people who are difficult to care for or who, though capable of self-care, are prone to disruptive behavior.

People on both sides of this controversy are outspoken in their views and consider it important to sway public opinion. Some patients—those who believe that medication helps them—agree with doctors that if more people used psychiatric drugs, thereby endorsing the premise that their condition has a physical basis, it would lessen the stigma traditionally attached to mental illness. In contrast, other people affected by mental ailments declare that, though they think and behave differently from "normal" people, there is no reason they should be required to change. The growing "mad pride" movement (which, in the eyes of its supporters, is analogous to the gay pride movement) asserts that people who are satisfied with their lives and do no harm to others should not be considered ill. Pointing out that until quite recently psychiatrists viewed homosexuality as a disorder, they say that there are no valid grounds for condemning schizophrenia; either. They want to be accepted for who they are rather than being judged according to majority views of who they ought to be.

In the middle of these extremes are the many defenders of human rights. According to this group, the question is not whether medication helps to heal or control mental illness but whether forcing it on people against their will violates their fundamental rights as human beings. A diagnosis of mental illness, they maintain, does not mean that a person is incapable of making decisions about his or her own care. If such an illness has a physical basis, there exists even greater reason that treatment should be voluntary: Society does not enforce treatment for other physical illnesses (with the exception of certain contagious diseases) on patients who do not want it. A report from the National Council on Disability in 2000, after presenting in detail the ways in which the civil rights of people with mental illnesses are customarily ignored, concludes, "Deprivation of human and civil rights cannot be tolerated in a country that was founded on the premise that everyone is created equal. The term 'liberty and justice for all' must be underscored and applied for people labeled with psychiatric disabilities."

Because they deal with civil rights, cases involving the treatment of patients with mental illness often come before the courts. To a lot of people, the need for the law to respect the right of every citizen to self-determination seems self-evident. Others, including many judges, interpret this "right" as the right to receive whatever care doctors believe is best. The Web site of the Treatment Advocacy Center declares that the mentally ill frequently do not receive the medical care they need because "misguided lawyers, too often misusing taxpayers' money, do all they can to block people who are too sick to know they are sick from getting treatment." Supporters of this view believe that medicating unwilling patients for their own good is of greater value to them than freedom of choice.

The situation is more complicated in the case of mentally ill prison inmates. Though the vast majority of people with mental illness are law-abiding citizens, some have been convicted of crimes, and prison officials feel justified in controlling inmates' objectionable behavior through forced medication. In the 2000 landmark case *Washington v. Harper*, the U.S. Supreme Court ruled six to three that coercion is permissible without a judicial hearing. There was strong dissent, however.

In that case, Walter Harper, who was in prison for robbery, had previously taken antipsychotic drugs but refused to continue taking them; he protested that he would "rather die" than take the medication and that the conditions under which the drugs were forcibly administered violated his due process rights under the Fourteenth Amendment to the Constitution.

The Washington State Supreme Court agreed, concluding that the "highly intrusive nature" of the treatment warranted greater procedural protections than had been provided. The U.S. Supreme Court majority, overruling the state court, averred,

> The extent of a prisoner's right under the [Due Process] Clause to avoid the unwanted administration of antipsychotic drugs must be defined in the context of the inmate's confinement. . . . The State has undertaken the obligation to provide prisoners with medical treatment consistent not only with their own medical interests, but also with the needs of the institution. . . . We hold that, given the requirements of the prison environment, the Due Process Clause permits the State to treat a prison inmate who has a serious mental illness with antipsychotic drugs against his will, if the inmate is dangerous to himself or others and the treatment is in the inmate's medical interest. . . . Notwithstanding the risks [of harmful side effects] that are involved, we conclude that an inmate's interests are adequately protected, and perhaps better served, by allowing the decision to medicate to be made by medical professionals rather than a judge.

Justice John Paul Stevens, in his dissenting opinion, wrote,

> Every violation of a person's bodily integrity is an invasion of his or her liberty. The invasion is particularly intrusive if it creates a substantial risk of permanent injury and premature death. Moreover, any such action is degrading if it overrides a competent person's choice to reject a specific form of medical treatment. And when the purpose or effect of forced drugging is to alter the will and the mind of the subject, it constitutes a deprivation of liberty in the most literal and fundamental sense. . . . The liberty of citizens to resist the administration of mind altering drugs arises from our Nation's most basic values.

> [The prison's] policy sweepingly sacrifices the inmate's substantive liberty interest to refuse psychotropic drugs, regard-

less of his medical interests, to institutional and administrative concerns. . . . Serving institutional convenience eviscerates the inmate's substantive liberty interest in the integrity of his body and mind. . . . A competent individual's right to refuse psychotropic medication is an aspect of liberty requiring the highest order of protection under the Fourteenth Amendment.

These conflicting opinions among the Supreme Court justices reflect the deep divide within society over the rights of people with mental illnesses. The gulf exists not only in relation to the issue of forced medicating, but also in relation to the question of involuntary institutionalization. The only area of widespread agreement is the belief that mental illness should not be stigmatized.

Parents Can Commit Children to Mental Institutions Without Their Consent

Case Overview

Parham v. J.R. (1979)

In 1975 attorneys from public service law firms brought suit on behalf of two Georgia children—identified only by their initials, J.L. and J.R.—to win their release from Central State Hospital in Georgia. The attorneys maintained that the children did not need to be institutionalized and that their original "voluntary" commitment, which was voluntary only on the part of the adults involved, was not valid.

J.L. was admitted to Central State when he was six years old at the request of his mother, who had remarried after her divorce from his father and had found J.L. uncontrollable. He had been expelled from school for that reason, and the admitting psychiatrist had diagnosed him as having a "hyperkinetic reaction of childhood." Two years later his mother and stepfather brought him home for a short time but still had problems, so they took him back to Central State, requesting his permanent admission and relinquishing their parental rights. Hospital employees recommended that he be placed in a foster home with "a warm, supported, truly involved couple," but the Department of Family and Children Services was unable to accomplish this goal.

The second child in the suit, J.R., had been declared a neglected child by the county and removed from his natural parents when he was three months old. He was placed in seven different foster homes in succession but was disruptive and incorrigible at school and could not conform to normal behavior patterns. When his seventh set of foster parents requested his removal from their home, the Department of Family and Children Services sought his admission to Central State, which he entered at the age of seven. The admission team determined that he was borderline retarded and suffered an "unsocialized, aggressive reaction of childhood." The team recommended unanimously that he be admitted, stating that he would "benefit from the structured environment" of the hospital and would "enjoy living and playing with boys of the same age." Later, additional unsuccessful efforts were made to place him in foster homes.

The district court that considered the case found that forty-six of the children at Central State could be better cared for in a less restrictive setting, such as a group home or foster home, if it were available. It held that institutionalization constitutes a severe deprivation of a child's liberty, which it defined in terms of freedom from the "emotional and psychic harm" caused by institutionalization, as well as freedom from bodily restraint. The court therefore ruled that the due process required for commitment includes the right to have the decision heard before an impartial tribunal.

The state of Georgia fought this decision all the way to the U.S. Supreme Court. (By this time J.L. had died, so only J.R. was listed in the case title.) The Supreme Court reversed the finding of the lower court and determined that no formal judicial hearing is required for the commitment of minors; in the Court's view, parents and psychiatrists can be counted on to make decisions in a child's best interests. The ruling states that "due process is not violated by use of informal, traditional medical investigative techniques."

> *"The statist notion that governmental power should supersede parental authority in all cases because some parents abuse and neglect children is repugnant to American tradition."*

The Court's Decision: Commitment of Minors to Mental Hospitals by Parents Is Not Unconstitutional

Warren Burger

Warren Burger was the chief justice of the U.S. Supreme Court from 1969 to 1986. He was a conservative who believed in a literal interpretation of the Constitution. In the following opinion in Parham v. J.R., *he presents the Court's reasons for deciding that parents can commit a child to a mental hospital without administrative hearings, which the district court had ruled was unconstitutional under the Due Process Clause of the Fourteenth Amendment. The Supreme Court reasoned that parents act in the best interests of their children and have the right to make decisions for them. The fact that a few parents abuse this right, Burger says, is no reason to require a hearing in all cases, which could delay necessary treatment and disrupt the relationship between parents and child. Although the Court agreed that a neutral fact-finder should participate in determining whether a child's hospitalization is medically justified, it felt that the admitting physician—and not an officer of the court—is best qualified for this role.*

Warren Burger, majority opinion, *James Parham et al. v. J. R. et al.*, U.S. Supreme Court, June 20, 1979.

The question presented in this appeal is what process is constitutionally due a minor child whose parents or guardian seek state administered institutional mental health care for the child, and, specifically, whether an adversary proceeding is required prior to or after the commitment.

Appellee J. R., a child being treated in a Georgia state mental hospital, was a plaintiff in this class action. . . . Appellee sought a declaratory judgment that Georgia's voluntary commitment procedures for children under the age of 18 violated the Due Process Clause of the Fourteenth Amendment, and requested an injunction against their future enforcement. . . .

After considering expert and lay testimony and extensive exhibits, and after visiting two of the State's regional mental health hospitals, the District Court held that Georgia's statutory scheme was unconstitutional because it failed to protect adequately the appellees' due process rights. . . .

The District Court's Decision

In holding unconstitutional Georgia's statutory procedure for voluntary commitment of juveniles, the District Court first determined that commitment to any of the eight regional hospitals constitutes a severe deprivation of a child's liberty. The court defined this liberty interest in terms of both freedom from bodily restraint and freedom from the "emotional and psychic harm" caused by the institutionalization. Having determined that a liberty interest is implicated by a child's admission to a mental hospital, the court considered what process is required to protect that interest. It held that the process due "includes at least the right after notice to be heard before an impartial tribunal."

In requiring the prescribed hearing, the court rejected Georgia's argument that no adversary-type hearing was required, since the State was merely assisting parents who could not afford private care by making available treatment similar to that offered in private hospitals and by private physicians. The court acknowledged that most parents who seek to have their children admitted to a state mental hospital do so in good faith. It, however, relied on one of appellees' witnesses who expressed an opinion that "some still look upon mental hospitals as a 'dumping ground.'" No specific evidence of such "dumping," however, can be found in the record.

The District Court also rejected the argument that review by the superintendents of the hospitals and their staffs was sufficient to protect the child's liberty interest. The court held that the inexactness of psychiatry, coupled with the possibility that the sources of information used to make the commitment decision may not always be reliable, made the superintendent's decision too arbitrary to satisfy due process. . . .

In an earlier day, the problems inherent in coping with children afflicted with mental or emotional abnormalities were dealt with largely within the family. Sometimes parents were aided by teachers or a family doctor. While some parents no doubt were able to deal with their disturbed children without specialized assistance, others, especially those of limited means and education, were not. Increasingly, they turned for assistance to local, public sources or private charities. Until recently, most of the states did little more than provide custodial institutions for the confinement of persons who were considered dangerous.

As medical knowledge about the mentally ill and public concern for their condition expanded, the states, aided substantially by federal grants, have sought to ameliorate [improve] the human tragedies of seriously disturbed children. Ironically, as most states have expanded their efforts to assist the mentally ill, their actions have been subjected to increasing litigation and heightened constitutional scrutiny. Courts have been required to resolve the thorny constitutional attacks on state programs and procedures with limited precedential guidance. In this case, appellees have challenged Georgia's procedural and substantive balance of the individual, family, and social interests at stake in the voluntary commitment of a child to one of its regional mental hospitals. . . .

The Interests of the Child

We must consider first the child's interest in not being committed. Normally, however, since this interest is inextricably linked with the parents' interest in and obligation for the welfare and health of the child, the private interest at stake is a combination of the child's and parents' concerns. Next, we must examine the State's interest in the procedures it has adopted for commitment and treatment of children. Finally, we must consider how well Georgia's procedures protect against arbitrariness in the decision to commit a child to a state mental hospital.

It is not disputed that a child, in common with adults, has a substantial liberty interest in not being confined unnecessarily for medical treatment, and that the state's involvement in the commitment decision constitutes state action under the Fourteenth Amendment. We also recognize that commitment sometimes produces adverse social consequences for the child because of the reaction of some to the discovery that the child has received psychiatric care.

This reaction, however, need not be equated with the community response resulting from being labeled by the state as delinquent, criminal, or mentally ill and possibly dangerous. The state, through its voluntary commitment procedures, does not "label" the child; it provides a diagnosis and treatment that medical specialists conclude the child requires. In terms of public reaction, the child who exhibits abnormal behavior may be seriously injured by an erroneous decision not to commit. Appellees overlook a significant source of the public reaction to the mentally ill, for what is truly "stigmatizing" is the symptomatology of a mental or emotional illness. The pattern of untreated abnormal behavior—even if nondangerous—arouses at least as much negative reaction as treatment that becomes public knowledge. A person needing, but not receiving, appropriate medical care may well face even greater social ostracism resulting from the observable symptoms of an untreated disorder.

However, we need not decide what effect these factors might have in a different case. For purposes of this decision, we assume that a child has a protectible interest not only in being free of unnecessary bodily restraints but also in not being labeled erroneously by some persons because of an improper decision by the state hospital superintendent.

The Interests of the Parents

We next deal with the interests of the parents who have decided, on the basis of their observations and independent professional recommendations, that their child needs institutional care. Appellees argue that the constitutional rights of the child are of such magnitude, and the likelihood of parental abuse is so great, that the parents' traditional interests in and responsibility for the upbringing of their child must be subordinated at least to the extent of providing a formal adversary hearing prior to a voluntary commitment.

Our jurisprudence historically has reflected Western civilization concepts of the family as a unit with broad parental authority over minor children. Our cases have consistently followed that course; our constitutional system long ago rejected any notion that a child is "the mere creature of the State" and, on the contrary, asserted that parents generally "have the right, coupled with the high duty, to recognize and prepare [their children] for additional obligations." *Pierce v. Society of Sisters, Wisconsin v. Yoder.* Surely, this includes a "high duty" to recognize symptoms of illness and to seek and follow medical advice. The law's concept of the family rests on a presumption that parents possess what a child lacks in maturity, experience, and capacity for judgment required for making life's difficult decisions. More important, historically it has recognized that natural bonds of affection lead parents to act in the best interests of their children.

As with so many other legal presumptions, experience and reality may rebut what the law accepts as a starting point; the incidence of child neglect and abuse cases attests to this. That some parents "may at times be acting against the interests of their children," as was stated in *Bartley v. Kremens*, creates a basis for caution, but is hardly a reason to discard wholesale those pages of human experience that teach that parents generally do act in the child's best interests. The statist [one who advocates high by centralized government control] notion that governmental power should supersede parental authority in all cases because some parents abuse and neglect children is repugnant to American tradition.

Nonetheless, we have recognized that a state is not without constitutional control over parental discretion in dealing with children when their physical or mental health is jeopardized. Moreover, the Court recently declared unconstitutional a state statute that granted parents an absolute veto over a minor child's decision to have an abortion. *Planned Parenthood of Central Missouri v. Danforth.* Appellees urge that these precedents limiting the traditional rights of parents, if viewed in the context of the liberty interest of the child and the likelihood of parental abuse, require us to hold that the parents' decision to have a child admitted to a mental hospital must be subjected to an exacting constitutional scrutiny, including a formal, adversary, pre-admission hearing.

Appellees' argument, however, sweeps too broadly. Simply because the decision of a parent is not agreeable to a child, or because it involves risks, does not automatically transfer the power to make that decision from the parents to some agency or officer of the state. The same characterizations can be made for a tonsillectomy, appendectomy, or other medical procedure. Most children, even in adolescence, simply are not able to make sound judgments concerning many decisions, including their need for medical care or treatment. Parents can and must make those judgments. Here, there is no finding by the District Court of even a single instance of bad faith by any parent of any member of appellees' class. We cannot assume that the result in *Meyer v. Nebraska* and *Pierce v. Society of Sisters* would have been different if the children there had announced a preference to learn only English or a preference to go to a public, rather than a church, school. The fact that a child may balk at hospitalization or complain about a parental refusal to provide cosmetic surgery does not diminish the parents' authority to decide what is best for the child. Neither state officials nor federal courts are equipped to review such parental decisions. . . .

The Interests of the State

The State obviously has a significant interest in confining the use of its costly mental health facilities to cases of genuine need. The Georgia program seeks first to determine whether the patient seeking admission has an illness that calls for inpatient treatment. To accomplish this purpose, the State has charged the superintendents of each regional hospital with the responsibility for determining, before authorizing an admission, whether a prospective patient is mentally ill and whether the patient will likely benefit from hospital care. In addition, the State has imposed a continuing duty on hospital superintendents to release any patient who has recovered to the point where hospitalization is no longer needed.

The State in performing its voluntarily assumed mission also has a significant interest in not imposing unnecessary procedural obstacles that may discourage the mentally ill or their families from seeking needed psychiatric assistance. The *parens patriae* [the power of the government to protect those legally unable to act for themselves] interest in helping parents care for the mental health of their children cannot be fulfilled if the parents are unwilling to take advantage of the opportunities because the admission process is too onerous, too embarrassing, or too contentious. It is surely not idle to speculate as to how many parents who believe they are acting in good faith would forgo state-provided hospital care if such care is contingent on participation in an adversary proceeding designed to probe their motives and other private family matters in seeking the voluntary admission.

The State also has a genuine interest in allocating priority to the diagnosis and treatment of patients as soon as they are admitted to a hospital, rather than to time-consuming procedural minuets before the admission. One factor that must be considered is the utilization of the time of psychiatrists, psychologists, and other behavioral specialists in preparing for and participating in hearings, rather than performing the task for which their special training has fitted them. Behavioral experts in courtrooms and hearings are of little help to patients.

The *amici* [friend of the court] brief of the American Psychiatric Association *et al.* points out that the average staff psychiatrist in a hospital presently is able to devote only 47% of his time to direct patient care. One consequence of increasing the procedures the state must provide prior to a child's voluntary admission will be that mental health professionals will be diverted even more from the treatment of patients in order to travel to and participate in—and wait for—what could be hundreds—or even thousands—of hearings each year. Obviously the cost of these procedures would come from the public moneys the legislature intended for mental health care.

Processes That Protect the Child's Rights

We now turn to consideration of what process protects adequately the child's constitutional rights by reducing risks of error without unduly trenching on traditional parental authority and without undercutting "efforts to further the legitimate interests of both the state and the patient that are served by" voluntary commitments. *Addington v. Texas*. We conclude that the risk of error inherent in the parental decision to have a child institutionalized for mental health care is sufficiently great that some kind of inquiry should be made by a "neutral factfinder" to determine whether the statutory requirements for admission are satisfied. That inquiry must carefully probe the child's background using all available sources, including, but not limited to, parents, schools, and other social agencies. Of course, the review must also include an interview with the child. It is necessary that the decisionmaker have the authority to refuse to admit any child who does not satisfy the medical standards for admission. Finally, it is necessary that the child's continuing need for commitment be reviewed periodically by a similarly independent procedure.

We are satisfied that such procedures will protect the child from an erroneous admission decision in a way that neither unduly burdens the states nor inhibits parental decisions to seek state help.

Due process has never been thought to require that the neutral and detached trier of fact be law trained or a judicial or administrative officer. Surely, this is the case as to medical decisions, for "neither judges nor administrative hearing officers are better qualified than psychiatrists to render psychiatric judgments." *In re Roger S.* (Clark, J., dissenting). Thus, a staff physician will suffice, so long as he or she is free to evaluate independently the child's mental and emotional condition and need for treatment.

It is not necessary that the deciding physician conduct a formal or quasi-formal hearing. A state is free to require such a hearing, but due process is not violated by use of informal, traditional medical investigative techniques. Since well established medical procedures already exist, we do not undertake to outline with specificity precisely what this investigation must involve. The mode and procedure of medical diagnostic procedures is not the business of judges. What is best for a child is an individual medical decision that must be left to the judgment of physicians in each case. We do no more than emphasize that the decision should represent an independent judgment of what the child requires and that all sources of information that are traditionally relied on by physicians and behavioral specialists should be consulted. . . .

Here, the questions are essentially medical in character: whether the child is mentally or emotionally ill, and whether he can benefit from the treatment that is provided by the state. While facts are plainly necessary for a proper resolution of those questions, they are only a first step in the process. In an opinion for a unanimous Court, we recently stated in *Addington v. Texas* that the determination of whether a person is mentally ill "turns on the *meaning* of the facts which must be interpreted by expert psychiatrists and psychologists."

The Problems with Administrative Hearings

Although we acknowledge the fallibility of medical and psychiatric diagnosis, we do not accept the notion that the shortcomings of specialists can always be avoided by shifting the decision from a trained specialist using the traditional tools of medical science to an untrained judge or administrative hearing officer after a judicial-type hearing. Even after a hearing, the nonspecialist decisionmaker must make a medical-psychiatric decision. Common human experience and scholarly opinions suggest that the supposed protections of an adversary proceeding to determine the appropriateness of medical decisions for the commitment and treatment of mental and emotional illness may well be more illusory than real.

Another problem with requiring a formalized, factfinding hearing lies in the danger it poses for significant intrusion into the parent-child relationship. Pitting the parents and child as adversaries often will be at odds with the presumption that parents act in the best interests of their child. It is one thing to require a neutral physician to make a careful review of the parents' decision in order to make sure it is proper from a medical standpoint; it is a wholly different matter to employ an adversary contest to ascertain whether the parents' motivation is consistent with the child's interests.

Moreover, it is appropriate to inquire into how such a hearing would contribute to the successful long-range treatment of the patient. Surely there is a risk that it would exacerbate whatever tensions already exist between the child and the parents. Since the parents can and usually do play a significant role in the treatment while the child is hospitalized, and even more so after release, there is a serious risk that an adversary confrontation will adversely affect the ability of the parents to assist the child while in the hospital. Moreover, it will make his subsequent return home more difficult. These unfortunate results are especially critical with an emotionally disturbed child; they seem likely to occur in the context of an adversary hearing in which the parents testify. A confrontation over such intimate family relationships would distress the normal adult parents, and the impact on a disturbed child almost certainly would be significantly greater.

It has been suggested that a hearing conducted by someone other than the admitting physician is necessary in order to detect instances where parents are "guilty of railroading their children into asylums" or are using "voluntary commitment procedures in order to sanction behavior of which they disapprov[e]." [James W.] Ellis. Curiously, it seems to be taken for granted that parents who seek to "dump" their children on the state will inevitably be able to conceal their motives, and thus deceive the admitting psychiatrists and the other mental health professionals who make and review the admission decision. It is elementary that one early diagnostic inquiry into the cause of an emotional disturbance of a child is an examination into the environment of the child. It is unlikely, if not inconceivable, that a decision to abandon an emotionally normal, healthy child and thrust him into an institution will be a discrete act leaving no trail of circumstances. Evidence of such conflicts will emerge either in the interviews or from secondary sources. It is unrealistic to believe that trained psychiatrists, skilled in eliciting responses, sorting medically relevant facts, and sensing motivational nuances will often be deceived about the family situation surrounding a child's emotional disturbance. Surely a lay, or even law-trained, factfinder would be no more skilled in this process than the professional.

By expressing some confidence in the medical decision-making process, we are by no means suggesting it is error-free. On occasion, parents may initially mislead an admitting physician, or a physician may erroneously diagnose the child as needing institutional care either because of negligence or an overabundance of caution. That there may be risks of error in the process affords no rational predicate for holding unconstitutional an entire statutory an administrative scheme that is generally followed in more than 30 states. . . .

In general, we are satisfied that an independent medical decisionmaking process, which includes the thorough psychiatric investigation described earlier, followed by additional periodic review of a child's condition, will protect children who should not be admitted; we do not believe the risks of error in that process would be significantly reduced by a more formal, judicial-type hearing.

> *"Notions of parental authority and family autonomy cannot stand as absolute and invariable barriers to the assertion of constitutional rights by children."*

Opinion Dissenting in Part: Children Committed to Mental Hospitals by Parents Are Entitled to Post-Admission Hearings

William Brennan

William Brennan was a justice of the U.S. Supreme Court from 1956 to 1990. He was an outspoken liberal and among the Court's most influential members. The following viewpoint is his dissenting opinion in Parham v. J.R., *in which he disagrees with the Court's ruling that no judicial hearing is necessary when parents wish to commit children to mental institutions. He says that because children have constitutional rights, he cannot accept the position that parents act in their children's best interest and therefore may waive children's due process rights. He maintains that it is not always true that parental decisions to institutionalize their children are in the children's best interests; even well-meaning parents lack the expertise to weigh the advantages and disadvantages of hospitalization, and uncertain diagnoses and medical caution often lead psychiatrists to recommend it when alternatives would be more beneficial. Because the prospect of judicial hearings might deter parents from seeking medical attention for their children and because hearings might pit the child*

William Brennan, opinion dissenting in part, *James Parham et al. v. J.R. et al.*, U.S. Supreme Court, June 20, 1979.

against the parents, says Justice Brennan, the hearing can legitimately be delayed until after admission. However, these considerations do not apply to post-admission hearings, and he considers it essential that such hearings be held.

I agree with the Court that the commitment of juveniles to state mental hospitals by their parents or by state officials acting *in loco parentis* [in place of parents] involves state action that impacts upon constitutionally protected interests, and therefore must be accomplished through procedures consistent with the constitutional mandate of due process of law. I agree also that the District Court erred in interpreting the Due Process Clause to require pre-confinement commitment hearings in all cases in which parents wish to hospitalize their children. I disagree, however, with the Court's decision to pretermit [disregard] questions concerning the post-admission procedures due Georgia's institutionalized juveniles. While the question of the frequency of post-admission review hearings may properly be deferred, the right to at least one post-admission hearing can and should be affirmed now. . . .

Rights of Children Committed to Mental Institutions

Commitment to a mental institution necessarily entails a "massive curtailment of liberty," *Humphrey v. Cady*, and inevitably affects "fundamental rights." Persons incarcerated in mental hospitals are not only deprived of their physical liberty, they are also deprived of friends, family, and community. Institutionalized mental patients must live in unnatural surroundings under the continuous and detailed control of strangers. They are subject to intrusive treatment which, especially if unwarranted, may violate their right to bodily integrity. Such treatment modalities may include forced administration of psychotropic medication, aversive conditioning, convulsive therapy, and even psychosurgery. Furthermore, as the Court recognizes, persons confined in mental institutions are stigmatized as sick and abnormal during confinement and, in some cases, even after release.

Because of these considerations, our cases have made clear that commitment to a mental hospital "is a deprivation of liberty which the State cannot accomplish without due process of law." *O'Connor v. Donaldson.* In the absence of a voluntary, knowing, and intelligent waiver, adults facing commitment to mental institutions are entitled to full and fair adversary hearings in which the necessity for their commitment is established to the satisfaction of a neutral tribunal. At such hearings, they must be accorded the right to "be present with counsel, have an opportunity to be heard, be confronted with witnesses against [them], have the right to cross-examine, and to offer evidence of [their] own." *Specht v. Patterson.*

These principles also govern the commitment of children. "Constitutional rights do not mature and come into being magically only when one attains the state-defined age of majority. Minors, as well as adults, are protected by the Constitution, and possess constitutional rights." *Planned Parenthood of Central Missouri v. Danforth.*

Indeed, it may well be argued that children are entitled to more protection than are adults. The consequences of an erroneous commitment decision are more tragic where children are involved. Children, on the average, are confined for longer periods than are adults. Moreover, childhood is a particularly vulnerable time of life, and children erroneously institutionalized during their formative years may bear the scars for the rest of their lives. Furthermore, the provision of satisfactory institutionalized mental care for children generally requires a substantial financial commitment that too often has not been forthcoming. Decisions of the lower courts have chronicled the inadequacies of existing mental health facilities for children.

In addition, the chances of an erroneous commitment decision are particularly great where children are involved. Even under the best of circumstances, psychiatric diagnosis and therapy decisions are fraught with uncertainties. These uncertainties are aggravated when, as under the Georgia practice, the psychiatrist interviews the child during a period of abnormal stress in connection with the commitment, and without adequate time or opportunity to become acquainted with the patient. These uncertainties may be further aggravated when economic and social class separate doctor and child, thereby frustrating the accurate diagnosis of pathology.

These compounded uncertainties often lead to erroneous commitments, since psychiatrists tend to err on the side of medical caution, and therefore hospitalize patients for whom other dispositions would be more beneficial. The National Institute of Mental Health recently found that only 36 of patients below age 20 who were confined at St. Elizabeths Hospital actually required such hospitalization. . . .

The Need to Limit Parents' Rights

Notwithstanding all this, Georgia denies hearings to juveniles institutionalized at the behest of their parents. Georgia rationalizes this practice on the theory that parents act in their children's best interests, and therefore may waive their children's due process rights. Children incarcerated because their parents wish them confined, Georgia contends, are really voluntary patients. I cannot accept this argument.

In our society, parental rights are limited by the legitimate rights and interests of their children. "Parents may be free to become martyrs themselves. But it does not follow they are free, in identical circumstances, to make martyrs of their children before they have reached the age of full and legal discretion when they can make that choice for themselves." *Prince v. Massachusetts*. This principle is reflected in the variety of statutes and cases that authorize state intervention on behalf of neglected or abused children and that, *inter alia* [among other things] curtail parental authority to alienate their children's property, to withhold necessary medical treatment, and to deny children exposure to ideas and experiences they may later need as independent and autonomous adults.

This principle is also reflected in constitutional jurisprudence. Notions of parental authority and family autonomy cannot stand as absolute and invariable barriers to the assertion of constitutional rights by children. States, for example, may not condition a minor's right to secure an abortion on attaining her parents' consent, since the right to an abortion is an important personal right and since disputes between parents and children on this question would fracture family autonomy.

This case is governed by the rule of [*Planned Parenthood of Central Missouri v.*] *Danforth*. The right to be free from wrongful incarceration, physical intrusion, and stigmatization has significance for the individual surely as great as the right to an abortion. Moreover, as in *Danforth*, the parent-child dispute at issue here cannot be characterized as involving only a routine childrearing decision made within the context of an ongoing family relationship. Indeed, *Danforth* involved only a potential dispute between parent and child, whereas here a break in family autonomy has actually resulted in the parents' decision to surrender custody of their child to a state mental institution. In my view, a child who has been ousted from his family has even greater need for an independent advocate.

Additional considerations counsel against allowing parents unfettered power to institutionalize their children without cause or without any hearing to ascertain that cause. The presumption that parents act in their children's best interests, while applicable to most childrearing decisions, is not applicable in the commitment context. Numerous studies reveal that parental decisions to institutionalize their children often are the results of dislocation in the family unrelated to the children's mental condition. Moreover, even well-meaning parents lack the expertise necessary to evaluate the relative advantages and disadvantages of inpatient, as opposed to outpatient, psychiatric treatment. Parental decisions to waive hearings in which such questions could be explored, therefore, cannot be conclusively deemed either informed or intelligent. In these circumstances, I respectfully suggest, it ignores reality to assume blindly that parents act in their children's best interests when making commitment decisions and when waiving their children's due process rights.

Postponement of Commitment Hearings

This does not mean States are obliged to treat children who are committed at the behest of their parents in precisely the same manner as other persons who are involuntarily committed. The demands of due process are flexible and the parental commitment decision carries with it practical implications that States may legitimately take into account. While, as a general rule, due process requires that commitment hearings precede involuntary hospitalization, when parents seek to hospitalize their children, special considerations militate in favor of postponement of formal commitment proceedings and against mandatory adversary pre-confinement commitment hearings.

First, the prospect of an adversary hearing prior to admission might deter parents from seeking needed medical attention for their children. Second, the hearings themselves might delay treatment of children whose home life has become impossible and who require some form of immediate state care. Furthermore, because adversary hearings at this juncture would necessarily involve direct challenges to parental authority, judgment, or veracity, pre-admission hearings may well result in pitting the child and his advocate against the parents. This, in turn, might traumatize both parent and child and make the child's eventual return to his family more difficult.

Because of these special considerations, I believe that States may legitimately postpone formal commitment proceedings when parents seek inpatient psychiatric treatment for their children. Such children may be admitted, for a limited period, without prior hearing, so long as the admitting psychiatrist first interviews parent and child and concludes that short-term inpatient treatment would be appropriate.

Georgia's present admission procedures are reasonably consistent with these principles. To the extent the District Court invalidated this aspect of the Georgia juvenile commitment scheme and mandated pre-confinement hearings in all cases, I agree with the Court that the District Court was in error.

I do not believe, however, that the present Georgia juvenile commitment scheme is constitutional in its entirety. Although Georgia may postpone formal commitment hearings, when parents seek to commit their children, the State cannot dispense with such hearings altogether. Our cases make clear that, when protected interests are at stake, the "fundamental requirement of due process is the opportunity to be heard 'at a meaningful time and in a meaningful manner.'" *Mathews v. Eldridge.* Whenever prior hearings are impracticable, States must provide reasonably prompt post-deprivation hearings.

The informal post-admission procedures that Georgia now follows are simply not enough to qualify as hearings—let alone reasonably prompt hearings. The procedures lack all the traditional due process safeguards. Commitment decisions are made *ex parte* [from a one-sided point of view]. Georgia's institutionalized juveniles are not informed of the reasons for their commitment; nor do they enjoy the right to be present at the commitment determination, the right to representation, the right to be heard, the right to be confronted with adverse witnesses, the right to cross-examine, or the right to offer evidence of their own. By any standard of due process, these procedures are deficient. I cannot understand why the Court pretermits condemnation of these *ex parte* procedures which operate to deny Georgia's institutionalized juveniles even "some form of hearing," *Mathews v. Eldridge*, before they are condemned to suffer the rigors of long-term institutional confinement.

Post-Admission Hearings

The special considerations that militate against pre-admission commitment hearings when parents seek to hospitalize their children do not militate against reasonably prompt post-admission commitment hearings. In the first place, post-admission hearings would not delay the commencement of needed treatment. Children could be cared for by the State pending the disposition decision.

Second, the interest in avoiding family discord would be less significant at this stage, since the family autonomy already will have been fractured by the institutionalization of the child. In any event, post-admission hearings are unlikely to disrupt family relationships. At later hearings, the case for and against commitment would be based upon the observations of the hospital staff and the judgments of the staff psychiatrists, rather than upon parental observations and recommendations. The doctors urging commitment, and not the parents, would stand as the child's adversaries. As a consequence, post-admission commitment hearings are unlikely to involve direct challenges to parental authority, judgment, or veracity. To defend the child, the child's advocate need not dispute the parents' original decision to seek medical treatment for their child, or even, for that matter, their observations concerning the child's behavior. The advocate need only argue, for example, that the child had sufficiently improved during his hospital stay to warrant outpatient treatment or outright discharge. Conflict between doctor and advocate on this question is unlikely to lead to family discord.

As a consequence, the prospect of a post-admission hearing is unlikely to deter parents from seeking medical attention for their children, and the hearing itself is unlikely so to traumatize parent and child as to make the child's eventual return to the family impracticable.

Nor would post-admission hearings defeat the primary purpose of the state juvenile mental health enterprise. Under the present juvenile commitment scheme, Georgia parents do not enjoy absolute discretion to commit their children to public mental hospitals. Superintendents of state facilities may not accept children for long-term treatment unless they first determine that the children are mentally ill and will likely benefit from long-term hospital care. If the superintendent determines either condition is unmet, the child must be released or refused admission, regardless of the parents' desires. No legitimate state interest would suffer if the superintendent's determinations were reached through fair proceedings with due consideration of fairly presented opposing viewpoints, rather than through the present practice of secret, *ex parte* deliberations.

Nor can the good faith and good intentions of Georgia's psychiatrists and social workers, adverted to by the Court, excuse Georgia's *ex parte* procedures. . . .

Rights of Children Committed by Their State Guardians

Georgia does not accord prior hearings to juvenile wards of the State of Georgia committed by state social workers acting *in loco parentis*. The Court dismisses a challenge to this practice on the grounds that state social workers are obliged by statute to act in the children's best interest.

I find this reasoning particularly unpersuasive. With equal logic, it could be argued that criminal trials are unnecessary, since prosecutors are not supposed to prosecute innocent persons.

To my mind, there is no justification for denying children committed by their social workers the prior hearings that the

Constitution typically requires. In the first place, such children cannot be said to have waived their rights to a prior hearing simply because their social workers wished them to be confined. The rule that parents speak for their children, even if it were applicable in the commitment context, cannot be transmuted into a rule that state social workers speak for their minor clients. The rule in favor of deference to parental authority is designed to shield parental control of child rearing from state interference. The rule cannot be invoked in defense of unfettered state control of child rearing or to immunize from review the decisions of state social workers. The social worker-child relationship is not deserving of the special protection and deference accorded to the parent-child relationship, and state officials acting *in loco parentis* cannot be equated with parents.

Second, the special considerations that justify postponement of formal commitment proceedings whenever parents seek to hospitalize their children are absent when the children are wards of the State and are being committed upon the recommendations of their social workers. The prospect of pre-admission hearings is not likely to deter state social workers from discharging their duties and securing psychiatric attention for their disturbed clients. Moreover, since the children will already be in some form of state custody as wards of the State, pre-hospitalization hearings will not prevent needy children from receiving state care during the pendency of the commitment proceedings. Finally, hearings in which the decisions of state social workers are reviewed by other state officials are not likely to traumatize the children or to hinder their eventual recovery.

For these reasons, I believe that, in the absence of exigent circumstances, juveniles committed upon the recommendation of their social workers are entitled to pre-admission commitment hearings. As a consequence, I would hold Georgia's present practice of denying these juveniles prior hearings unconstitutional.

Children incarcerated in public mental institutions are constitutionally entitled to a fair opportunity to contest the legitimacy of their confinement. They are entitled to some champion who can speak on their behalf and who stands ready to oppose a wrongful commitment. Georgia should not be permitted to deny that opportunity and that champion simply because the children's parents or guardians wish them to be confined without a hearing. The risk of erroneous commitment is simply too great unless there is some form of adversary review. And fairness demands that children abandoned by their supposed protectors to the rigors of institutional confinement be given the help of some separate voice.

> *"It's gratifying to have this affirmation that of course parents care, that of course they try to act in their offspring's best interest, and that of course they know what's good for their children."*

In *Parham* the Court Recognized That Parents Act in Their Children's Best Interests

Joan Beck

Joan Beck was a nationally syndicated columnist for the Chicago Tribune. *In the following viewpoint she expresses her approval of the Supreme Court's decision in* Parham v. J.R., *which established that parents can commit a minor child to a mental institution without a court hearing. She asserts that popular psychology and militant advocates of children's rights have gone too far in tarnishing the image of parents, and she views the Court's ruling as a welcome change. Beck says that she is especially cheered by the way the opinion was worded, because it emphasized the view that parents know what is best for a child.*

The image of parents has been tarnished lately by statistics on child abuse and neglect, by promoters of child-free lifestyles, by militant advocates of children's rights, and by a new cycle of pop-psych books laying a sort of all-purpose blame on mom and/or dad.

Joan Beck, "Court Says Parents, of All People, Have Rights," *Chicago Tribune*, June 25, 1979, p. C2. Copyright © 1979 Chicago Tribune Company. All rights reserved. Reproduced by permission.

So the off-hand pat on the back parents got last week [June 1979] from the Supreme Court comes as a welcome bit of burnishing. And it might be an indication that the high court does not intend to keep chipping away at parental rights and responsibilities, as it seems to have been doing in recent years. (A case in point: *Planned Parenthood of Missouri v. Danforth*, which held that a minor could obtain an abortion without a parent's knowledge or permission.)

The current decision in *Parham v. J.R.* overturns an appellate court ruling that it is unconstitutional for parents to commit a minor child to a mental institution for treatment without a formal adversary court hearing before admission to assure the child the right to due process.

The court noted that the state (Georgia in this case and Pennsylvania in an associated case) does not permit parents just to dump a child on a mental hospital on their own. Medical findings that the youngster needs treatment and should benefit from hospitalization are necessary for admission. Doctor and staff reassess both diagnosis and progress at short, regular intervals. Hospitals must discharge a patient immediately when he recovers or if treatment is no longer considered useful.

The onus for making sure no child is institutionalized unnecessarily already falls heavily on the hospital. And the court noted it's "unlikely if not inconceivable" that parents could push an emotionally normal, healthy child into an institution without being detected.

What isn't required, the court decided, is to put parents through an adversary hearing before their child can get treatment—a laying-the-blame kind of legal procedure that would delay getting help and might turn parents away from even trying.

An Encouraging Opinion

What's particularly cheering, however, is how the court worded its opinion.

"The law's concept of the family rests on a presumption that parents possess what a child lacks in maturity, experience, and capacity for judgment required for making life's difficult decisions," wrote Chief Justice Warren E. Burger, for the majority. "Historically, it has recognized that natural bonds of affection lead parents to act in the best interests of their children."

Burger noted that child abuse and neglect do occur. But this, he said, "is hardly a reason to discard wholesale those pages of human experience that teach that parents generally do act in the child's best interests. . . . The statist notion that governmental power should supersede parental authority in all cases because some parents abuse and neglect children is repugnant to American tradition."

Burger also wrote, "Simply because the decision of a parent is not agreeable to a child or because it involves risks does not automatically transfer the power to make that decision from the parents to some agency or officer of the state . . . Most children, even in adolescence, simply are not able to make sound judgments concerning many decisions, including their need for medical care or treatment. Parents can and must make those judgments."

The court also noted, refreshingly, that informal, traditional medical procedures might work better in safeguarding an emotionally disturbed or retarded child than an adversary hearing.

Legal probing to "ascertain whether the parent's motivation is consistent with the child's interest" could upset the "critical parent-child relationship," Burger said.

Parents have been bad-mouthed so much by so many for so long. It's gratifying to have this affirmation that of course parents care, that of course they try to act in their offspring's best interest, and that of course they know best what's good for their children—from the highest court in the land.

> "The same safeguards should be afforded mature minors as are afforded adults in involuntary commitment hearings."

Mature Minors Are Not Adequately Protected from Erroneous Commitment to Mental Hospitals

Linda V. Tiano

At the time this paper was written, Linda V. Tiano was a student at the Boston University School of Law. In the following viewpoint she argues that the Supreme Court in Parham v. J.R. *should have distinguished between mature minors—those old enough to understand the nature and consequences of medical treatment—and younger children. She states that in earlier cases, it has made this distinction, and that it is not clear why it failed to do so when deciding whether parents could commit children to mental institutions against their will. The commitment of minors is called "voluntary" because it is voluntary on the part of the parents, but Tiano holds that it is not voluntary in the case of mature minors, and that they should have the same legal protections given to adults who are involuntarily committed. She also points out that the Court should not have concluded that staff physicians qualify as neutral fact-finders in deciding whether minors should be committed, because they often are biased in favor of hospitalization and may be under pressure both from parents and from hospitals to admit more patients.*

Linda V. Tiano, "Parham v. J.R.: 'Voluntary' Commitment of Minors to Mental Institutions," *American Journal of Law and Medicine*, Spring 1980, p. 134–39, 142–47, 149. Reproduced by permission.

At one time parents had an almost absolute right to control their children. Until a child reached the age of majority, he or she lacked legal capacity to consent to medical care; if the parents did not consent, the person who treated the minor child could be liable for battery.

In recent years, the law has moved away from the rule that parents must consent before their children may receive medical treatment. Courts have held, for instance, that mature minors may authorize treatment for themselves. A mature minor [writes Eve W. Paul] is "one who is sufficiently intelligent and mature to understand the nature and consequences of the medical treatment being sought." In determining whether the minor is sufficiently mature to understand the treatment and to consent to it, relevant factors to be considered include the age, intelligence, maturity, experience, economic independence, general conduct as an adult and freedom from the control of parents, "the risk involved in the particular procedure," [Paul] and "whether the proposed treatment is for the benefit of the child, and is done with a purpose of saving his life or limb." [*Bonner v. Moran*] The mature minor exception to the parental-consent requirement has been characterized as an extension of the rule requiring that physicians obtain "informed consent" from all patients before undertaking treatment.

Courts have applied the mature minor doctrine to medical treatment in general and to sex-related medical treatment, such as obtaining contraceptives and abortions, in particular. In *Planned Parenthood of Central Missouri v. Danforth*, the Supreme Court held that a parent may not overrule a mature minor's decision to have an abortion if she consents after consultation with her physician. The Court extended this ruling in *Bellotti v. Baird*, which was decided shortly after *Parham*. In *Bellotti*, the Court held that a statute that required no more than parental consultation prior to obtaining an abortion also violated minors' constitutional rights. These cases indicate that where bodily autonomy is concerned, a third party may not interfere with decisions made by mature minors and their physicians.

The mature minor doctrine, as applied in *Danforth* and *Bellotti*, indicates that mature minors are legally competent, under certain circumstances, to give informed consent to treatment. Although the issue in those cases was whether the minor could consent, and not whether her consent was required before an abortion could be performed, an abortion performed on a mature minor against her wishes probably would be unlawful. One state court case, *In re Smith*, explicitly dealt with this issue, and held that a statute permitting a mature minor to consent to an abortion implicitly forbids compelling the minor to have one. Thus, when the mature minor doctrine is applicable, the minor's consent not only is sufficient to authorize treatment, but should be required before treatment may begin.

Applying the Mature Minor Doctrine to Voluntary Commitment

The Supreme Court's analysis of minors' consent to treatment in *Danforth* and *Bellotti* should have been used to distinguish between mature and immature minors in determining the appropriate procedural safeguards in *Parham*. Despite the young age of the two named plaintiffs, the certified class in the suit included all minors under eighteen years of age. Thus, the Court's decision is equally applicable to all minors, regardless of maturity.

The *Parham* Court distinguished the *Danforth* abortion statute from the Georgia voluntary commitment statute on the grounds that the abortion statute had permitted an absolute parental veto over the minor's abortion decision. The *Parham* Court explained that while parents in Georgia have broad discretion to apply for the hospitalization of their children, they in no sense have an absolute right to commit their children to a state mental hospital because the Georgia statute requires the chief medical officer to exercise "independent" judgment about the child's need for confinement.

The Court's distinction of the Georgia statute from *Danforth*'s abortion statute should not be applicable to mature minors. Although the Georgia statute does not permit parents to make a wholly arbitrary decision, it does place decision-making power regarding institutionalization in the hands of parents and of the hospital's chief medical officer. The mature minor doctrine, however, recognizes that mature minors have an independent right to authorize treatment. This right is violated whether a parent or a physician is permitted to substitute his or her own judgment for that of the minor. . . .

Parham is inconsistent with another Supreme Court decision, *Kremens v. Bartley*, which recognized the distinction between mature and immature minors in the context of voluntary commitment to mental institutions. In *Kremens*, a district court declared the Pennsylvania voluntary commitment statute unconstitutional. Subsequently, the Pennsylvania legislature amended the statute so that adolescents over the age of fourteen would be in the same position as adults for purposes of voluntary admissions to mental institutions. On appeal, the Supreme Court held that the case was moot in light of the amendment to the statute, since all of the named plaintiffs were over fourteen years old. In dicta [material that is merely informative or explanatory], the Court commented that the Pennsylvania legislature, in amending the statute, had recognized the different interests of older and younger juveniles. . . .

Furthermore, the Georgia statute challenged in *Parham* implicitly recognizes the distinction between mature and immature minors. Although the statute permits parents and guardians to apply for the admission of minors of any age into mental hospitals, it also permits children twelve and older to volunteer themselves for mental health treatment, provided that the consent of a parent or guardian also is obtained. The

Georgia legislature apparently believed that minors twelve and older are mature enough to give informed consent to hospitalization for mental illness. Permitting the parents alone to consent to hospitalization for these mature minors, however, is inconsistent with characterizing the commitment as "voluntary." Commitment is not voluntary where the person committed legally is capable of consenting but has not done so. While the Georgia statute allows a mature minor to consent to his or her own commitment, it does not permit the same minor to forbid commitment by a third party. A person who has the right to consent also must have the "right to forbid." . . .

In light of prior Supreme Court decisions and of the Georgia statute itself, therefore, the *Parham* Court should have found not only that mature minors are competent to consent to commitment for mental illness, but also that they must consent before the commitment can be characterized as voluntary. Confinement of an adult in a mental institution without that person's consent is considered involuntary, and stringent procedural protections are required before the person may be committed. Similarly, institutionalization of a mature minor who legally is competent, but unwilling to consent to treatment also should be considered involuntary. The same safeguards should be afforded mature minors as are afforded adults in involuntary commitment hearings. These safeguards should include an opportunity to be heard before a judge or administrative hearing officer, and the requirement that clear and convincing evidence of mental illness be presented before the person may be hospitalized. . . .

Requirement of a Neutral Factfinder

The *Parham* Court's holding that a neutral factfinder is necessary and sufficient as it applies to immature minors committed by their parents is consistent with previous Supreme Court decisions. Prior cases have held that minors do possess constitutional due process rights, but that these rights are not always as broad as those of adults. Minors, therefore, may not be entitled to the same procedural protections as adults.

In *Goss v. Lopez*, for example, the Supreme Court held that while minors are entitled to procedural due process protections before being suspended from public school, an informal discussion between school authorities and the student prior to suspension will suffice. The Supreme Court held in *In re Gault* that a minor facing a juvenile court proceeding that could result in incarceration is entitled to an adversary hearing. Since suspension from school is a lesser deprivation of liberty than incarceration, more stringent procedural protections are required in juvenile court proceedings than in school disciplinary proceedings.

A minor's interest in avoiding improper institutionalization probably falls between the interests represented by *Goss v. Lopez* and *In re Gault.* . . .

The *Parham* Court held that a minor is entitled to an independent determination by a neutral factfinder. Given the investigatory responsibilities of a neutral factfinder, this procedure affords greater protection than an informal discussion, but is not as stringent as an adversary hearing. Therefore, with respect to immature minors committed by their parents, the Court correctly held that a neutral factfinder is sufficient to protect the liberty interests of minors.

The Physician as a Neutral Factfinder

Although the *Parham* Court was correct in holding that a neutral factfinder is necessary to afford minors due process, it erroneously concluded that a staff physician qualifies as a neutral factfinder. A staff physician may not be able to make a truly independent decision, an essential element of the Court's definition of a neutral factfinder.

Although the Supreme Court stated that the factfinder must be "independent," the Court did not clearly state what "independent" means in this context. In *Goldberg v. Kelly*, the Supreme Court stated that where an independent decision maker was required, prior involvement in the case would not necessarily preclude independence, but that the decision maker actually should not have made the determination under review. When a parent applies for the admission of a child to a mental institution pursuant to a voluntary commitment statute, the staff physician not only is participating in the decision, but in reality, is making the decision. The admitting physician should not be considered a neutral factfinder capable of reviewing the commitment decision.

In addition, staff physicians may be subjected to strong pressures from parents who are applying for the admission of their child to commit the child. The physician interviews both the parents and the child, but where their statements conflict, the physician will tend to identify with and believe the parents. The physician will be closer in age to the parents, may have similar values, and may have children of his or her own, all of which may cause the physician to feel sympathy for and identify with the role of a parent. The identification makes it difficult for the physician to objectively examine the parents' decision to hospitalize their child.

The physician also may be subjected to other pressures to commit patients. If a hospital has empty beds, the physician may commit patients who are not in need of hospitalization. In addition, psychiatrists tend to overdiagnose so as not to permit a possible illness to go untreated. The staff physician, therefore, is not a neutral factfinder as defined by the Court.

The *Parham* Court should have considered the use of third parties who would more closely approximate the Court's definition of a neutral factfinder. Law review commentary suggests the appointment of legal counsel upon the minor's admission to the hospital. The attorney would determine whether the family or guardian is making a bona fide attempt to seek treatment for the child and whether the child is in need of treatment. If the child is not in need of treatment, the attorney then would assist the child in obtaining his or her release. Mandatory conferences between the child and a psychiatrist who is not affiliated with the hospital also have been suggested. All of these proposals involve the appointment of a disinterested third party to meet with the child and determine if the child is in need of treatment. The ability of legal counsel to determine the need for treatment, however, is questionable, as most attorneys have no mental health training. Mandatory conferences with an independent psychiatrist are of limited value unless the psychiatrist investigates the child's background and has authority to challenge the admission. In addition, most psychiatrists may not be willing to contradict the opinion of a fellow psychiatrist.

In order to introduce a truly neutral factfinder into the admission procedure, this note suggests the appointment of independent mental health professionals who actually would meet the Court's definition of a neutral factfinder. The independent mental health professional would not be a psychiatrist and would not make a medical diagnosis, but instead would be a social worker or child case worker who is trained to explore and to investigate the child's environment and to interpret the child's behavior in light of that environment. The independent professional would investigate the minor's family and school environments and interview the minor and the family. The staff physician still would be responsible for making the medical diagnosis of mental illness, but such a diagnosis would not lead to voluntary commitment unless the independent professional agreed that hospitalization was an appropriate form of treatment. Since the parents would not hire or choose the independent professional, he or she would be free from parental pressure to commit the minor. The professional also would be free from pressure from the hospital to fill beds, since he or she would not be a hospital employee. Additionally, an independent mental health professional would be in a better position to recommend alternatives to hospitalization, such as foster home placement.

The independent professional also could decide if the minor is mature. If so, the minor's consent would be necessary for voluntary commitment. If the minor is immature, and the staff physician believes that the minor is in need of treatment, the independent professional would determine whether hospitalization is in the minor's best interests, taking into consideration the physician's recommendation, as well as the minor's home and school environment. If the independent professional believes that hospitalization is not in the minor's best interests, the minor could not be committed under a voluntary commitment statute, but could be committed only by the adversarial involuntary commitment process. . . .

Procedures developed on a state by state basis . . . are not likely to be sufficient to protect the liberty interests of all minors who are committed under voluntary commitment statutes. Requiring more stringent procedures under the fourteenth amendment due process clause would have been both appropriate and desirable. For now, however, minors must rely on inadequate procedural protection from "voluntary," indefinite, and possibly erroneous commitment to mental institutions.

Forcibly Medicating Psychiatric Patients

Case Overview

Rogers v. Okin (1980); *Mills v. Rogers* (1982); *Rogers v. Commissioner* (1983)

The most contentious issue with regard to mental illness concerns whether individuals diagnosed as mentally ill can be forcibly drugged. Some people, including most but not all psychiatrists, believe that antipsychotic medications are beneficial and that it is justifiable to force them on people for their own good. Others believe that overriding a patient's will is an intolerable violation of fundamental human rights. They consider it an unqualified evil to administer mind-altering drugs without a patient's consent for any reason other than to prevent violence toward others. The majority of patients who refuse medication do so because the drugs can have adverse consequences on mood and the capacity to think and also often produce devastating physical effects—sometimes permanent ones. Patients' rights advocates believe that the patient should decide whether the desired effects are worth the undesirable ones.

The first court decision to establish a mentally competent patient's right to refuse medication was *Rogers v. Okin* (the name was changed to *Mills v. Rogers* when it was taken to the U.S. Supreme Court and again to *Rogers v. Commissioner* when it was finally decided by the Massachusetts Supreme Court). Rubie Rogers was the lead plaintiff in a group of patients who sued Boston State Hospital in Massachusetts because of ill treatment. The federal district court trial lasted seventy-two days and produced a transcript more than eight thousand pages long, along with more than two thousand pages of post-trial briefs. There was extensive testimony about the damaging effects of psychiatric drugs, some of it from Rogers.

At the trial's conclusion Judge Joseph Tauro ruled that except in emergencies, involuntarily confined mental patients, like all other patients, have a right to make decisions about treatment and may not be forcibly drugged. If a patient has been judged by a court to be mentally incompetent to make decisions, then a guardian must be appointed and there must be a judicial hearing to determine whether forcible drugging will be allowed.

The ruling was appealed to the federal circuit court, which upheld the district court's opinion but modified it to the extent of allowing patients to be drugged against their will not only to prevent physical harm to themselves or others, but also to prevent immediate and permanent deterioration of their mental condition. The case was then appealed to the U.S. Supreme Court. However, after the Court agreed to hear it and before the oral argument took place, another case was decided in Massachusetts that affected state laws concerning mental patients. Therefore, the Court did not decide the case but sent it back to the circuit court for reconsideration in the light of the Massachusetts case, and that court remanded it to the Supreme Court of Massachusetts for final resolution. The Massachusetts court agreed with the original circuit court decision, emphasizing that "To protect the incompetent person within its power, the state must recognize the dignity and worth of such a person and afford to that person the same panoply of rights and choices it recognizes in competent persons."

> *"A person has a constitutionally pro-*
> *tected interest in being left free by the*
> *state to decide for himself whether to*
> *submit to the serious and potentially*
> *harmful medical treatment that is*
> *represented by the administration of*
> *antipsychotic drugs."*

The Circuit Court's Opinion: Patients with Mental Illness Can Refuse Medication Except in Emergencies

Frank M. Coffin

Frank M. Coffin became a judge of the U.S. Court of Appeals for the First Circuit in 1965 and was its chief judge from 1972 to 1983. Previously, he was a member of the U.S. House of Representatives. In the following opinion in the landmark case Rogers v. Okin, *Coffin states that the parties agree that a "normal" person has a constitutional right to refuse potentially harmful treatment with antipsychotic drugs but that such drugs can be forcibly administered to mentally ill persons to prevent them from harming others. State officials, however, have asserted that the lower court's definition of emergencies is too narrow and that the state should also be allowed to give drugs by force to patients who are merely potentially violent. The lower court ruled that this cannot be done unless the patient has been declared legally incompetent to make decisions about treatment and that incompetent patients are entitled to a court hearing. Coffin states that*

Frank M. Coffin, opinion, *Rubie Rogers et al. v. Robert Okin M.D. et al*, U.S. Court of Appeals for the First Circuit, November 25, 1980.

the Court of Appeals agrees that the definition of emergencies should be widened to include situations in which immediate administration of drugs is necessary to keep a patient's condition from getting worse.

We begin our analysis with what seems to us to be an intuitively obvious proposition: a person has a constitutionally protected interest in being left free by the state to decide for himself whether to submit to the serious and potentially harmful medical treatment that is represented by the administration of antipsychotic drugs. The precise textual source in the Constitution of the protection of this interest is unclear, and the authorities directly supportive of the proposition itself are surprisingly few. Nevertheless, we are convinced that the proposition is correct and that a source in the Due Process Clause of the Fourteenth Amendment for the protection of this interest exists, most likely as part of the penumbral right to privacy, bodily integrity, or personal security.

None of the parties or amici [friends of the court; people who volunteer information to help the court make its decision] in this suit contest the correctness of this general proposition. With regard to the treatment of the mentally ill in state run institutions, however, defendants point to several state interests that, they claim, override the individual's protected interest and justify the forced administration of drugs. Additionally, defendants contend that within this context, the interests of the individuals to whom the state wishes to administer drugs are fundamentally different from those of individuals who are not mentally ill, and are not in fact inconsistent with the interests of the state. Plaintiffs, on the other hand, while conceding that the interests of the individual are not absolute and can be overridden in certain circumstances, argue that the mere fact that an individual suffers from mental illness and resides in a mental health facility does not constitute such a circumstance. In order to resolve this dispute between the parties, we first examine the various state interests involved.

As we have indicated, neither defendants nor their amici argue that the state could forcibly administer antipsychotic drugs to a randomly selected "normal" individual. Unfortunately, the plaintiffs in this suit are far from "normal." Instead, suffering from various mental illnesses, they are in the words of the district court "victims of fate shortchanged by life." As a result of their afflictions, they are in many instances in desperate need of care and treatment, and, in some cases, are dangerous to either themselves or others. Because of their illnesses, some of these individuals are unable to make any meaningful choice as to whether they should accept treatment, including the administration of drugs. Given these circumstances, the state asserts primarily its police power and its parens partiae power [power of the state to help those legally unable to act for themselves] as justifications for the forcible administration of antipsychotic drugs to those individuals who are in state run hospitals as a result of mental illness.

Police Power

The parties agree that the state has a legitimate interest in protecting persons from physical harm at the hands of the mentally ill. They also agree that this interest can justify the forcible administration of drugs to a mentally ill person whether or not that person has been adjudicated incompetent to make his own treatment decisions. The district court accordingly held that "a committed mental patient may be forcibly medicated in an emergency situation in which a failure to do so would result in a substantial likelihood of physical harm to that patient, other patients, or to staff members of the institution." Plaintiffs have no complaint with this ruling. Defendants, however, have two basic complaints, which they raise on this appeal. First, defendants contend that the district court's definition of emergency is too narrow and should include situations in which "a patient requires the prompt initiation of medication to prevent further suffering by that patient or the rapid worsening of that person's clinical state." . . .

Defendants' second basic complaint is that the necessity of finding a "substantial likelihood of physical harm . . ." is an overly rigid and unworkable requirement. Defendants argue that some mentally ill patients have an identifiable capacity for spontaneous acts of violence but that it is not always possible to determine beforehand whether a specific patient is likely to commit such acts. This problem of prediction is increased, defendants claim, by the prospect that doctors will be second-guessed in section 1983 suits for damages. In sum, defendants assert that the overall effect of following the district court's standard is to increase the incidence of violent acts that otherwise would not occur had a less restrictive standard been used.

The district court rejected this complaint, finding that the actual experience of operating under the standard during the period covered by a temporary restraining order showed defendants' "gloomy forecast" to be "more dramatic than factual". To a certain extent it is clear that throughout this litigation defendants and their supporting amici have erroneously attributed acts of violence to the strictness of the court's standard. Nevertheless, it does appear that the district court may have overlooked or misconstrued evidence of specific acts of violence occurring as a result of defendants' difficulty in applying the court's standard. . . .

There are two sets of interests, each capable of being compelling and, most importantly, each capable of varying from case to case. On the institutional side, we deal with an institution to which many individuals are involuntarily committed because of a demonstrated proclivity for committing acts of violence outside the hospital community, a proclivity that the record shows often carries over after commitment. The volatility of a large concentration of such individuals adds substance and immediacy to the state's concern in preventing violence. This concern takes on an added dimension when we consider that patients themselves are the likely victims of any violence. These mental patients are persons who, as we have noted, have "a right, under the Fourteenth Amendment, to be secure in (their) life and person while confined under state authority." *Harper v. Cserr.* On the individual's side, we deal with the concededly substantial right of competent patients to be free from the forcible administration of antipsychotics, the violation of which right may not only occasion temporary distress but possibly aftereffects as well. . . .

The array of relevant factors bearing on a quantitative judgment in this institutional setting almost defies prediction or reviewability. For example, we suspect that the likelihood of a violence-prone patient's losing control of himself may often depend on the provocation of others. The difficulty of factoring such possibilities into an individual determination makes a preponderance prediction fall short of being practical, not to mention short of being constitutionally mandated.

In so holding, we do not imply that the Constitution places no limits on the discretion of the defendants. The state's purpose in administering drugs forcibly must be to further its police power interests, i.e., the decision must be the result of a determination that the need to prevent violence in a particular situation outweighs the possibility of harm to the medicated individual. Thus, medication cannot be forcibly administered solely for treatment purposes absent a finding of incompetency. Additionally, reasonable alternatives to the administration of antipsychotics must be ruled out. Otherwise, the administration of the drugs would not be necessary to accomplish the state's objective. Indeed, it may be possible that in most situations less restrictive means will be available. . . . Finally, given the interests involved, the Fourteenth Amendment requires the imposition of procedures whereby the necessary determinations can be made with due process. . . .

In sum, we hold that the district court should not attempt to fashion a single "more-likely-than-not" standard as a substitute for an individualized balancing of the varying interests of particular patients in refusing antipsychotic medication against the equally varying interests of patients and the state in preventing violence. Because we recognize the legitimacy of both of these interests, we conclude that neither should be allowed necessarily to override the other in a blanket fashion. Instead, the court should leave this difficult, necessarily ad hoc balancing to state physicians and limit its own role to designing procedures for ensuring that the patients' interests in refusing antipsychotics are taken into consideration and that antipsychotics are not forcibly administered absent a finding by a qualified physician that those interests are outweighed in a particular situation and less restrictive alternatives are unavailable.

Parens Patriae Powers

The concept of parens patriae, which developed with reference to the power of the sovereign to act as "the general guardian of all infants, idiots, and lunatics" [*Hawaii v. Standard Oil*], is clearly applicable to the facts of this case. There is no doubt that "(t)he state has a legitimate interest under its parens patriae powers in providing care to its citizens who are unable to care for themselves. . . ." The use of these powers to go beyond the mere protection of the mentally ill from harm to the forcible administration of treatment thought curative is regarded as having its origins in the Massachusetts case of *In re Oates*. Such use of the powers is implicit in their very nature.

"Inherent in an adjudication that an individual should be committed under the state's parens patriae power is the decision that he can be forced to accept the treatments found to be in his best interest; it would be incongruous if an individual who lacks the capacity to make a treatment decision could frustrate the very justification for the state's action by refusing such treatments." . . .

The state today finds its interest in being able to offer meaningful assistance to the individual even more substantial than it was in previous times. However, for the state to invoke this interest as a justification for the administration of treatment that could represent substantial intrusions upon the individual, the individual himself must be incapable of making a competent decision concerning treatment on his own. Otherwise, the very justification for the state's purported exercise of its parens patriae power—its citizen's inability to care for himself, would be missing. Therefore, the sine qua non [essential element] for the state's use of its parens patriae power as justification for the forceful administration of mind-affecting drugs is a determination that the individual to whom the drugs are to be administered lacks the capacity to decide for himself whether he should take the drugs.

For the most part, the parties do not contest this conclusion. Instead, their dispute concerns whether or not such a determination has in fact been properly made with respect to the plaintiffs. . . .

Under the statutory scheme any given individual might have been committed despite the fact that he competently believed that treatment was not in his best interests.

Defendants contest the correctness of this conclusion by pointing to the fact that the statutory scheme does require a finding that the committed individual suffers from mental illness. This finding, defendants argue, is a sufficient predicate to state action based on its parens patriae power. Nothing in the statutory scheme, however, suggests that a finding of mental illness is equivalent to a finding that the individual is incapable of deciding for himself whether commitment and treatment are in his own best interest. Indeed, as the district court noted, the fact that Massachusetts law provides for a separate proceeding for determinations of legal incompetency, strongly implies that the commitment proceeding itself is not intended to be a determination that the individual lacks the capacity to make his own treatment decisions. This implication is explicitly confirmed in another section of the statute that recognizes the ability and right of a committed patient to refuse electroconvulsion treatment and lobotomies. Finally, as a factual matter, the district court found, and defendants concede, that not all patients institutionalized for mental illness are incapable of making their own treatment decisions.

The foregoing analysis is not intended to suggest that the Massachusetts commitment scheme is unconstitutional. To the contrary, in many respects the Massachusetts scheme goes well beyond the minimum requirements mandated by the Fourteenth Amendment. The point of our analysis is instead to demonstrate that the commitment decision itself is an inadequate predicate to the forcible administration of drugs to an individual where the purported justification for that action is the state's parens patriae power. . . .

Emergency Situations

We do agree with defendants, however, that there are two aspects of the district court's ruling that require some modification. First, the district court held that absent an "emergency" defendants can never forcibly medicate an individual without an adjudication of incompetency and approval by the appointed guardian. The court defined an emergency as "circumstances in which a failure to (forcibly medicate) would bring about a substantial likelihood of physical harm to the patient or others." In so restricting the definition to instances in which immediate action is required to prevent physical harm the district court rejected defendants' claim that an emergency should also include situations in which the immediate administration of drugs is reasonably believed to be necessary to prevent further deterioration in the patient's mental health.

The district court did not proffer any explanation for requiring an actual adjudication of incompetency in such circumstances. While judicial determinations are certainly preferable in general, room must be left for responsible state officials to respond to exigencies that render totally impractical recourse to traditional forms of judicial process. "The judicial model of fact finding for all constitutionally protected interests, regardless of their nature, can turn rational decisionmaking into an unmanageable enterprise." *Parham v. J.R.*

Moreover, in the particular situation presented here, it cannot be said that the interests of the patient himself would be furthered by requiring responsible physicians to stand by and watch him slip into possibly chronic illness while awaiting an adjudication of incompetency. Instead, the interests of the individual in such a situation coincide with those of the state and mandate decisive, immediate action. We therefore vacate the district court's limited definition of the emergency circumstances in which adjudications are not required and remand the case for consideration of alternative means for making incompetency determinations in situations where any delay could result in significant deterioration of the patient's mental health.

Second, it is possible to read the district court's opinion as implying that once a determination of incompetency has been made, a traditional, individual guardian must make all treatment decisions involving the use of antipsychotic drugs. To the extent that the district court's opinion might be so read, we reject that part of its holding.

The district court focused extensively on the harmful side effects that the various medications can produce. Its findings concerning these effects are supported by the record. However, the record also shows that in many situations, despite the risks of harmful side effects, the administration of drugs to an individual is clearly in his best interests because of the beneficial effects that the drugs can have, including the amelioration of the patient's illness. In such situations, the failure to medicate an incompetent patient could have side effects—e.g., the unnecessary and possibly irreversible continuation of his illness—far more harmful, and probable, than any that might result from the drugs themselves.

Thus, any treatment decision, including the decision not to treat, brings with it the potential for serious harm to the patient. Accordingly, if we were to adopt what is arguably the district court's reasoning concerning guardians, we would be led to the conclusion that appellants must consult a guardian whenever they decide not to administer drugs to an incompetent patient. Such a requirement would, we think, be impractical and largely incapable of enforcement. . . .

In so holding, we do not imply that the Constitution places no limits whatsoever on the manner in which the state may decide how to treat incompetent patients. Following a determination of incompetency, state actions based on parens patriae interests must be taken with the aim of making treatment decisions as the individual himself would were he competent to do so. Furthermore, in order to ensure compliance with this requirement, some minimum procedural requirements would seem to be necessary. . . .

Appellants claim that they employ such procedures, and ask us to declare them sufficient. We hesitate, however, to make such a finding. Despite our intensive review of this case, our familiarity with the factual details of the functioning of the hospitals and the needs of the patients does not approach that of the district court. Moreover, neither the district court nor the parties have had the opportunity to evaluate the present procedures in terms of the criteria we set forth today. For the purposes of this appeal, we therefore rest on our holding that, absent an emergency, a judicial determination of incapacity to make treatment decisions must be made before the state may rely on its parens patriae powers to forcibly medicate a patient, but, as a constitutional matter, the state is not required to seek individualized guardian approval for decisions to treat incompetent patients with antipsychotic drugs. . . .

Voluntary Patients

One point that our analysis leaves unaddressed is whether patients who voluntarily enter a state mental health facility have a right to refuse antipsychotic medication. The district court held that "the voluntary patient has the same right to refuse treatment in a non-emergency as does the involuntary patient." The court apparently rejected defendants' argument that voluntary patients can be forced to choose between leaving the hospital and accepting prescribed treatment.

In so holding, the district court in effect found that Massachusetts citizens have a constitutional right upon voluntary admittance to state facilities to dictate to the hospital staff the treatment that they are given. The district court cited no authority for this finding, and we know of none. Massachusetts law provides for the voluntary admission of mental health patients who are "in need of care and treatment . . . providing the admitting facility is suitable for such care and treatment." The statute does not guarantee voluntary patients the treatment of their choice. Instead, it offers a treatment regimen that state doctors and staff determine is best, and if the patient thinks otherwise, he can leave. We can find nothing even arguably unconstitutional in such a statutory scheme. . . .

In conclusion, we find it worth noting that in an important respect this case differs from the traditional, adversary model of private litigation. Plaintiffs and defendants, as well as the various amici, share in large part the primary goal of assuring that adequate care and treatment are provided to patients in state hospitals. As is evident from this opinion, we have not accepted absolutist positions advanced by either the parties or amici.

> *"There was substantial evidence in this case that these drugs can blunt the consciousness, impair cognition, learning ability, problem-solving ability."*

Lawyers Debate Whether Benefits of Antipsychotic Medication Outweigh the Dangers

Stephen Schultz and Richard Cole

Stephen Schultz was the attorney who represented the state of Massachusetts and hospital officials in the case of Rogers v. Okin, *which was renamed* Mills v. Rogers *when appealed to the U.S. Supreme Court. Richard Cole was the attorney who represented Rubie Rogers and other mental patients. In the following excerpt from their argument before the Supreme Court, they present their differing views on antipsychotic medication. Schultz argues that such medication is necessary for most mental patients, that it is effective even when forcibly administered, and that their illness, not the drugs, is mind-altering. Cole argues that these drugs are dangerous and that patients should be free to reject them. They have devastating effects on mental processes, and furthermore, he says, in many patients they cause an irreversible and untreatable physical illness called tardive dyskinesia, which impairs muscle control, speech, swallowing, and all other motor activity. After hearing the argument the Supreme Court*

Stephen Schultz and Richard Cole, oral argument, *Mark J. Mills et al. v. Rubie Rogers et al.*, U.S. Supreme Court, January 13, 1982.

did not decide the case; because of the possible effect of another recent case on Massachusetts law, it sent the case back to be reconsidered by the lower courts.

Stephen Schultz: Mr. Chief Justice, and may it please the Court, in argument today [January 13, 1982], I would like to focus on what the defendants believe to be the two fundamental reasons that there is no constitutional right to refuse treatment.

First would be that allowing one patient to refuse treatment is necessarily going to negatively impair the state's ability to perform its legitimate objective of maintaining order in its hospitals, and second of all, of treating those patients who are not themselves refusing treatment.

In other words, what I am saying is that to allow one patient to refuse treatment, there will necessarily be an increase of violence in our institutions.

The First Circuit talks about allowing forced medication for emergency situations, but they simply do not focus on the fact of the unpredictability of violence in mentally ill patients, the impulsivity of violent acts, the fact that mental patients are acting upon irrational thoughts, and that this simply cannot always be predicted.

The second—

Unidentified Justice: Well, they did give you a broader mandate than Judge Tauro [the District Court judge] had done, didn't they?

Mr. Schultz: There is no doubt that the First Circuit opinion in our mind is less wrong than the district court opinion.

I could say that maybe less people will be hurt under the First Circuit opinion than would be hurt under the district court opinion. I hardly feel that justifies the opinion.

The second point that I want to make as to this first fundamental reason is that if you allow one patient to remain in your hospital in a deteriorated state, this is going to affect the health of other patients, whether or not there is violence.

A hospital is a milieu setting, and if you have patients who are deteriorated, this will set off the illnesses of other patients, and I will talk about this more later.

The second major point that I want to discuss in argument today which we believe to be a second fundamental reason is that we suggest that the original decision to commit an individual against his will for treatment purposes when it is known at the time that the patient is committed that antipsychotic medications are a necessary part of the treatment of the vast majority of the seriously mentally ill acts as a sufficient predicate for the later administration of this medication against the patient's will after the commitment.

In other words, let me just reword what we consider this basic argument to be all about.

There is no determination of incompetency at the time that a patient is committed, yet the state is empowered, despite this lack of a finding of incompetency, is empowered to commit an individual against his will for treatment.

We suggest similarly without any finding of incompetency the state should be empowered to carry out that treatment against the patient's will which was ordered at the time of commitment.

The Importance of Medication

In order to fully understand these two fundamental arguments that we believe necessitate there being a finding of no right to refuse treatment, I think it is first necessary to focus very, very briefly on what exactly is the role of antipsychotic medications in our state hospitals.

The record in this case is clear that antipsychotic medications are a necessary part of the treatment for the vast majority of seriously mentally ill patients.

Unidentified Justice: Do those drugs have a component of tranquilizer in them?

Mr. Schultz: They do, but they are not very good tranquilizers. You shouldn't use them and it wouldn't be proper practice to use them as a tranquilizer.

They are a poor tranquilizer, and to the extent that they do tranquilize, the sedative effects wear off in two or three weeks.

If you want to tranquilize, there are other drugs which are tranquilizers.

We are talking about a specific group of patients, and it must be recognized, and that group of patients are patients who are so seriously mentally ill that they could be committed, plus it is acceptable medical practice to use antipsychotic medications for those patients.

Unidentified Justice: Mr. Schultz, do you disagree with the district court's findings about the drugs themselves, that they are mind-altering and they have significant side effects and so forth?

Mr. Schultz: I certainly disagree with the finding that they are mind-altering. What they do is restore a chemical imbalance in the brain to the original balance. It is the psychosis that is mind-altering, as I think a very cogent article points out.

The non-conformist treated of his illness, the psychotic non-conformist will remain a non-conformist. A conformist treated of his illness will remain a conformist. They don't alter the mind. The psychosis alters the mind.

As for the effects, the side effects, there are side effects, but simply put, the state's position, and I think the First Circuit so found, is that the dangers of psychosis untreated are far greater than the dangers of any of these side effects. . . .

A point which the defendants want to emphasize is not only is the record clear that these medications are effective when taken voluntarily; the record is also overwhelming that these medications are effective when forcibly administered, the district court's finding notwithstanding.

There is no way . . . To argue that these drugs are not administered . . . are not effective when administered forcibly simply ignores the tens of case histories in this case of patients who refused antipsychotic medication and deteriorated, and then against their will were forcibly medicated and improved, and there is simply no explanation for that other than the fact that these are chemicals, and they make the brain . . . they restore an imbalance, and this balance is restored whether or not a person voluntarily takes these medications or whether a person is forced to take these medications.

Let me turn to what the Commonwealth feels is another very important point in this case, and that is the recognition that we are talking about seriously mentally ill individuals, as the patients who have been given the right to refuse medication, and specifically, what do we know about the serious mental illness which is sufficient to commit an individual?

We know that an acutely psychotic patient is terrorized, in a state of panic, unbearable agony, pain, and distress. That is undisputed in the record.

We know that schizophrenic patients, which are the majority of patients for whom it would be a proper practice to give antipsychotic medications, don't think rationally, that they think on their own autistic terms.

We know that a classic symptom of mental illness which leads these patients to being committed is ambivalence, including ambivalence to treatment.

We know that . . . it is undisputed in the record that many, many patients who were forcibly medicated in the past, after they were forcibly medicated, thanked the doctors for forcibly medicating them when they weren't speaking their own true mind. . . .

Antipsychotic Medications Are Dangerous

Unidentified Justice: [To Richard Cole] Tell me what you object to in the medical decision.

I don't suppose the doctors involved are just interested in giving medication willy-nilly. There is a range of reasons that they use, I suppose. What reasons do you particularly object to?

Mr. Cole: Well, if I can first begin to answer by saying that the first thing we take is that these drugs are extremely dangerous drugs.

Unidentified Justice: I understand that.

Mr. Cole: These are not relatively risk-free drugs.

And what we are saying is, in an individual who is not dangerous, that means, the doctor does not believe there is a potential for harm in the institution, number one, and who is not causing the kind of security problems which belong to the police power—

Unidentified Justice: So why is he giving it?

Mr. Cole: Then he is only giving it in order to what they believe to benefit the individual, to have them improve their health in the institution, and it is our view that the state—

Unidentified Justice: And you suggest that even if those are the reasons, and valid ones, nevertheless the patient should be, if he is competent, should be able to say, sorry, I don't care to take it?

Mr. Cole: That's right.

That is particularly important in this case, because we are not talking about relatively risk-free drugs.

We are talking about a drug which the district court found that 30 to 50 percent of the patients are getting a syndrome called tardive dyskinesia, which is the deforming, often irreversible and untreatable symptom that causes patients to have facial contortions and grimaces, to have lip-smacking and tongue protrusions that can't be controlled by the patient, that when this syndrome gets fully manifested patients find that they cannot speak, that ... and speech becomes incomprehensible, swallowing and breathing are impaired as well as all motor activity.

Now, if this was only 1 or 2 or 3 percent of the patient population involved—

Unidentified Justice: So the patient, if he is competent, should say, well, I would rather be the way I am than be that other way.

Mr. Cole: That's correct, and we are saying that ... we are not saying this for all treatment. We are saying that there are particular types of treatment, such as psychosurgery, electroshock, that raise such fundamental interests in terms of what these drugs can do.

The petitioners say these drugs don't affect the mind. Well, the district court found ... there was substantial evidence in this case ... that these drugs can blunt the consciousness, impair cognition, learning ability, problem-solving ability.

Unidentified Justice: Mr. Cole, none of the plaintiffs in this case suffered any of these effects, did they?

Mr. Cole: That is not correct, Your Honor.

There were admissions given ... the distinction that is being drawn is between the main plaintiffs and the class of patients, where there was substantial evidence dealing with both, and there was admissions concerning the effects of these drugs, and doctors admitted that some patients had from these drugs in the class, had clouded consciousness.

Unidentified Justice: Not 25 to 50 percent of the class.

You didn't mean to say that, did you?

Mr. Cole: No, in terms of tardive dyskinesia, which is the side effect, the only ... they agree that many patients had tardive dyskinesia in admissions.

The only specific evidence they had—

Unidentified Justice: What do you mean by many?

Mr. Cole: There was no ... in the—

Unidentified Justice: Because I got the impression from the district court's finding that this is a very serious possible side effect, but the actual litigants, at least the named plaintiffs, you are right, had not suffered that.

Mr. Cole: We only raised it for one named plaintiff, Your Honor.

Unidentified Justice: That it is a danger, but one that didn't materialize very often within this class.

Mr. Cole: On one ward, the testimony they had in specifics of one ward in the hospital during one period where a defense witness, a doctor who worked there, testified that 10 to 15 patients out of 70 to 75 patients on that ward had clear cases of tardive dyskinesia.

That is a 20 percent rate of patients who have tardive dyskinesia, clear cases. We are not talking about subtle signs of tardive dyskinesia. The testimony was clear cases of tardive dyskinesia. So that there was evidence for the district court.

The district court also used the medical literature and the expert testimony, and there was a lot of national experts who testified about what is the general rate of patients who are getting this deforming, disabling syndrome, and—

Unidentified Justice: Would it not be correct that when a patient gets that . . . is in that unfortunate group, that somebody has made a medical misjudgment?

Mr. Cole: No, Your Honor. Any patient who gets antipsychotic drugs is at risk.

The problem with these . . . I mean, one of the problems is, not only do the drugs cause tardive dyskinesia, but they can also mask the development of the syndrome, that means, the manifestations of the syndrome, initially, so often by the time the doctor finds out, even using the best medical standards, by the time the doctor finds out that the patient has the syndrome, it is often irreversible, often untreatable. Not always, but often. So, we are not talking about if there is bad practices.

Unidentified Justice: The difficulty with your argument that I see, at least, is that the more difficult it is to accurately appraise the risk, it seems to me the less wisdom there is in saying that the layman should make the medical judgment.

Mr. Cole: What we are saying is, is that the patient is the one who has to assume the risk of this irreversible side effect, and a competent individual should, just like other competent adults in our society—

Unidentified Justice: But even a competent doctor apparently can't appraise it accurately.

Mr. Cole: Well, the question is not whether . . . one can competently say that 20 to 50 percent of patients over the long term who are taking these drugs are getting tardive dyskinesia. That is a risk that one can understand.

One can't selectively say that this particular patient is going to get it. Just like when someone has an operation and the doctor says there is a one in 100 chance of death, they don't know if specifically that one person is going to be the person who is going to die. Of course, that person wouldn't take the therapy.

Unidentified Justice: Well, and of course this doesn't show up until there has been medication over a prolonged period of time, as I recall.

Mr. Cole: Well, the record reflects that within three months of antipsychotic drug treatment, there have been reports that patients have had tardive dyskinesia. Within a year of antipsychotic drug treatment, the patient is at high risk.

Now, you have to remember that a number of these patients have been on antipsychotics in the past. We are not talking about one year straight. We are talking about one year.

Eighty-five percent of the patient population are either chronic patients or patients who are being readmitted to the hospital who have had prior hospitalizations, and therefore have take antipsychotic drugs, so the risk is great for that 85 percent immediately if they have had any history of antipsychotic drugs.

Unidentified Justice: But you would apply the same procedures Justice White asked you about where the man is dangerous to himself and so forth, you would apply the same procedure whether the patient has ever had the drug before or whether he has been using it for ten years.

Mr. Cole: That's correct, because that is not the only side effect that a patient experiences.

Unidentified Justice: No, but this is the more serious one, as I understand.

Mr. Cole: Well, it is the one that in terms of permanent affect is there, but there are a number of other . . . a patient can experience a number of side effects that last the course of being on antipsychotic drug treatment, very painful syndromes, disabling, not only of the body but also of the mind.

And what we are saying is that the tradition in our society has been a competent individual has the right, even if we believe it is wrong, to refuse treatment as long as . . . and in this situation we are talking about extremely dangerous treatment, and we believe that there is a liberty interest involved, and the court of appeals attempted to weigh the strong patient's interest and the institutional interest, and we feel that the weighing was responsible giving due deference to the state and the institutional needs, but at the same time recognizing dangers of these drugs and the important patient's interest in being able to refuse, especially considering that we are really talking about and focusing on patients who the Supreme Judicial Court of Massachusetts says are competent to make these rational treatment decisions.

"Since it is the patient who ... must suffer the consequences of any treatment decision, the patient has the right to make that decision."

Massachusetts Court's Opinion: Incompetent Patients with Mental Illness Have the Same Rights as Other Patients

Ruth Abrams

Ruth Abrams was the first female justice of the Supreme Judicial Court of Massachusetts, where she served from 1978 until her retirement in 2000. The following is the opinion of that court on Rogers v. Okin *(renamed* Rogers v. Commissioner *for this appeal), which finally settled the case after many years of litigation. In it Abrams points out that the fact that someone has been committed to a mental institution does not necessarily mean that person is incompetent to make decisions about whether to accept medication, and individuals not judged legally incompetent in a separate proceeding have the right to forego treatment even when this seems unwise to medical professionals. This right must extend to incompetent patients, she says, because the value of human dignity extends to them. The guardian of such a patient must seek a "substituted judgment" by a court, based not on what doctors believe is in that patient's best interests, but on what he or she would have decided if competent. She lists the factors the judge must take into account in making this determination. Finally, she discusses forced medication in emergency*

Ruth Abrams, opinion, *Rubie Rogers et al. v. Commissioner of the Department of Mental Heath et al.*, Supreme Judicial Court of Massachusetts, November 29, 1983.

situations. When this is done to protect others, she says, the laws concerning the use of chemical restraints must be obeyed.

We are asked to respond to nine questions certified by the United States Court of Appeals for the First Circuit which focus on the right of involuntarily committed mental patients to refuse treatment, and the standards and procedures which must be followed to treat those patients with antipsychotic medication. The basic conclusions we reach are that a committed mental patient is competent and has the right to make treatment decisions until the patient is adjudicated incompetent by a judge. If a patient is adjudicated incompetent, a judge, using a substituted judgment standard, shall decide whether the patient would have consented to the administration of antipsychotic drugs. No State interest justifies the use of antipsychotic drugs in a non-emergency situation without the patient's consent. Antipsychotic drugs, which are used to prevent violence to third persons, to prevent suicide, or to preserve security, are being used as chemical restraints and must follow the strictures of [the law,] and the regulations promulgated pursuant to the statute. A patient may be treated with antipsychotic drugs against his will and without prior court approval to prevent the "immediate, substantial, and irreversible deterioration of a serious mental illness." If a patient is medicated in order to avoid "immediate, substantial, and irreversible deterioration of a serious mental illness," and the doctors expect to continue to treat the patient with antipsychotic medication over the patient's objection, the doctors must seek adjudication of incompetency, and, if the patient is adjudicated incompetent, the court must formulate a substituted judgment treatment plan. . . .

Competence of Some Patients to Make Decisions

Questions 1, 2, and 3. Competence of involuntarily committed patients to make treatment decisions; judicial determination of incompetence. "No person shall be deemed to be incompetent to manage his affairs, to contract, to hold professional or occupational or vehicle operators licenses or to make a will solely by reason of his admission or commitment in any capacity to the treatment or care of the [Mental Health] department or to any public or private facility." A judge may order the civil commitment of a person after a hearing only if he finds that the person is mentally ill and that the person's failure to be committed would create a likelihood of serious harm. The Legislature defined "[l]ikelihood of serious harm" as "(1) a substantial risk of physical harm to the person himself as manifested by evidence of threats of, or attempts at, suicide or serious bodily harm; (2) a substantial risk of physical harm to other persons as manifested by evidence of homicidal or other violent behavior or evidence that others are placed in reasonable fear of violent behavior and serious physical harm to them; or (3) a very substantial risk of physical impairment or injury to the person himself as manifested by evidence that such person's judgment is so affected that he is unable to protect himself in the community and that reasonable provision for his protection is not available in the community." There is no requirement that a person be incompetent in order to be committed.

The first two definitions of likelihood of serious harm "provide no adjudication of judgmental capacity; commitment is based on a determination of risk of physical harm to the individual or to others." *Rogers [v. Okin].* Put simply, such a commitment is for public safety purposes and does not reflect lack of judgmental capacity. The third definition, although more relevant to the person's judgmental abilities, says nothing concerning his competence to make treatment decisions. A person may be competent to make some decisions, but not others. Furthermore, as the Court of Appeals noted, there is no way to pinpoint those patients committed under the third definition. Thus, "under the statutory scheme any given individual might have been committed despite the fact that he competently believed that treatment was not in his best interests." In addition, the Federal District Court judge found that most patients "are able to appreciate the benefits, risks, and discomfort that may reasonably be expected from receiving psychotropic medication."

A determination of incompetence, on the other hand, is made by a judge who appoints a guardian only after he finds the person "incapable of taking care of himself by reason of mental illness." Thus, the statutes, as worded, comprehend the competence of an involuntarily committed mental patient to make treatment decisions. The fact that [the law] expressly authorizes patients to refuse psychosurgery and electroconvulsive treatment does not, as the defendants assert, exclude by implication the patients' rights to make treatment decisions as to antipsychotic drugs. The right of an individual "to manage his own person" necessarily encompasses the right to make basic decisions with respect to "taking care of himself," *Fazio v. Fazio*, including decisions relating to the maintenance of physical and mental health. We think it clear that the right to make treatment decisions is an essential element of the patient's general right "to manage his affairs." "[A] finding [of incompetence], apart from evidence as to mental illness, should consist of facts showing a proposed ward's inability to think or act for himself as to matters concerning his personal health, safety, and general welfare. . . ." Absent such a finding, a person is competent to "act for himself as to matters concerning his personal health," including acceptance or refusal of medication. Thus, a person diagnosed as mentally ill and committed to a mental institution is still considered to be competent to manage his personal affairs.

We conclude that a mental patient has the right to make treatment decisions and does not lose that right until the patient is adjudicated incompetent by a judge through incompetence proceedings. . . .

The defendants argue that they, as doctors, should be responsible for making treatment decisions for involuntarily committed patients, whether competent or not. We do not agree. "Every competent adult has a right 'to forego treatment, or even cure, if it entails what for him are intolerable consequences or risks however unwise his sense of values may be in the eyes of the medical profession.'" *Harnish v. Children's Hosp. Medical Center.* This right has constitutional and common law origins, which protect each person's "strong interest in being free from nonconsensual invasion of his bodily integrity." *Superintendent of Belchertown State School v. Saikewicz.* Since by statute and by common law, involuntarily committed patients are competent until adjudicated incompetent, and because we have held that competent individuals have a right to refuse treatment, the defendants' argument fails.

We conclude that a distinct adjudication of incapacity to make treatment decisions (incompetence) must precede any determination to override patients' rights to make their own treatment decisions. Other courts have drawn similar conclusions. . . .

The Decision to Treat Incompetent Patients

Questions 4 and 5. The decision to treat incompetent mental patients with antipsychotic drugs. In Massachusetts there is "a general right in all persons to refuse medical treatment in appropriate circumstances. The recognition of that right must extend to the case of an incompetent, as well as a competent, patient because the value of human dignity extends to both. . . . To protect the incompetent person within its power, the State must recognize the dignity and worth of such a person and afford to that person the same panoply of rights and choices it recognizes in competent persons." *Superintendent of Belchertown State School v. Saikewicz.* Further, "if an incompetent individual refuses antipsychotic drugs, those charged with his protection must seek a judicial determination of substituted judgment." *Guardianship of Roe.*

A substituted judgment decision is distinct from a decision by doctors as to what is medically in the "best interests" of the patient. "[T]he goal is to determine with as much accuracy as possible the wants and needs of the individual involved." *Superintendent of Belchertown State School v. Saikewicz.* The decision "should be that which would be made by the incompetent person, if that person were competent, but taking into account the present and future incompetency of the individual as one of the factors which would necessarily enter into the decision-making process of the competent person," and giving "the fullest possible expression to the character and circumstances of that individual." Use of the substituted judgment standard is not unique to Massachusetts. The decision is not simply a question whether treatment is to be rendered, but also may entail a choice between alternative treatments. The doctor must offer treatment to the involuntarily committed patient, but, since it is the patient who bears the risks as well as the benefits of treatment by antipsychotic drugs, and must suffer the consequences of any treatment decision, the patient has the right to make that decision. In short, treatment decisions are the patient's prerogative solely.

"[O]ur prior cases have established that prior judicial approval is required before a guardian may consent to administering or withholding of proposed extraordinary medical treatment." *Matter of Moe.* Since we have decided that treatment with antipsychotic drugs is such an extraordinary treatment, we necessarily conclude that court approval is mandatory before forcible medication of an incompetent patient with those drugs in a nonemergency situation can take place.

The amici [friends of the court] American Psychiatric Association and Massachusetts Psychiatric Society, arguing on behalf of the psychiatric profession, urge us not to require a substituted judgment by a judge for institutionalized incompetent mentally ill patients. They assert that if a substituted judgment is required before there can be forcible medication of involuntarily confined, incompetent patients, the decision as to substituted judgment should be made by a qualified physician and not a judge. This procedure, the so called medical model, would, the doctors claim, protect the incompetent patient's civil rights to refuse treatment, while providing the hospital with a qualified person who can make the substituted judgment decision at the hospital. The medical model is also advantageous, the doctors claim, because it provides flexibility and avoids the adversary quality of judicial proceedings. The doctors thus conclude that if a substituted judgment is required, the medical model is the appropriate procedure for this court to follow. We do not agree. "No medical expertise is required [for making the substituted judgment decision], although medical advice and opinion is to be used for the same purposes and sought to the same extent that the incompetent individual would, if he were competent." *Guardianship of Roe.*

The only relevant fact which differs between *Guardianship of Roe* and this case is that the incompetent patient in *Guardianship of Roe* was not institutionalized. The defendants argue that the mere fact of institutionalization and the needs of the hospital should be sufficient to transfer the treatment decision authority from the judge to the doctors. "[I]f the doctrines of informed consent and right of privacy [that underlie the substituted judgment determination] have as their foundations the right to bodily integrity, and control of one's own fate, then those rights are superior to the institutional considerations." *Superintendent of Belchertown State School v. Saikewicz.*

In *Guardianship of Roe* and *Matter of Spring*, we outlined the various factors to be considered in determining whether a judicial substituted judgment decision is required. Five of these discussed in *Guardianship of Roe* were "(1) the intrusiveness of the proposed treatment, (2) the possibility of adverse side effects, (3) the absence of an emergency, (4) the nature and extent of prior judicial involvement, and (5) the like-lihood of conflicting interests."

The fact that a patient has been institutionalized and de-clared incompetent brings into play the factor of the likeli-hood of conflicting interests. The doctors who are attempting to treat as well as to maintain order in the hospital have inter-ests in conflict with those of their patients who may wish to avoid medication. . . .

The Substituted Judgment Treatment Decision

We conclude that, if a patient is declared incompetent, a court must make the original substituted judgment treatment deci-sion and should approve a substituted judgment treatment plan. After adjudication of an involuntarily committed patient as incompetent, the judge may conduct a hearing on the ap-propriate treatment to be administered. The parties "must be given adequate notice of the proceedings, an opportunity to be heard in the trial court, and to pursue an appeal." *Matter of Moe*. To this end, a guardian ad litem [advocate for the pa-tient] should be appointed, and the opinions of experts gath-ered so that all views are available to the judge. The judge may delegate to a guardian the power to monitor the treatment process to ensure that the substituted judgment treatment plan is followed.

At least six factors must be considered by the judge in ar-riving at the substituted judgment decision. "In this search, procedural intricacies and technical niceties must yield to the need to know the actual values and preferences of the ward." *Guardianship of Roe*. These six factors are detailed in *Guard-ianship of Roe*, and we briefly restate them here.

First, the judge must examine the patient's "expressed preferences regarding treatment." If made while competent, such a preference "is entitled to great weight" unless the judge finds that the patient would have changed his opinion after reflection or in altered circumstances. Even if he lacked the capacity to make his treatment decisions at the time, his expressed preference "must be treated as a critical factor in the determination of his 'best interests,'" since it is the patient's true desire that the court must ascertain.

Second, the judge must evaluate the strength of the incompetent patient's religious convictions, to the extent that they may contribute to his refusal of treatment. "[T]he question to be addressed is whether certain tenets or practices of the incompetent's faith would cause him individually to reject the specific course of treatment proposed for him in his present circumstances. . . . While in some cases an individual's beliefs may be so absolute and unequivocal as to be conclusive in the substituted judgment determination, in other cases religious practices may be only a relatively small part of the aggregated considerations." *Guardianship of Roe.*

Third, the impact of the decision on the ward's family must be considered. In *Guardianship of Roe*, we indicated that this factor is primarily relevant when the patient is part of a closely knit family. The consideration of impact on the family includes the cost in money and time that the family must bear, together with any desire of the patient to minimize that burden. In addition, a patient may be faced with "two treatments, one of which will allow him to live at home with his family and the other of which will require the relative isolation of an institution." The judge may then consider what affection and assistance the family may offer. However, the judge must be careful to ignore the desires of institutions and persons other than the incompetent "except in so far as they would affect his choice."

Fourth, the probability of adverse side effects must be considered. This includes an analysis of "the severity of these side effects, the probability that they would occur, and the circumstances in which they would be endured."

Fifth, the prognosis without treatment is relevant to the substituted judgment decision. It is probable that most patients would wish to avoid a steadily worsening condition. However, the judge must again reach an individualized, subjective conclusion regarding this factor, after examining it from the "unique perspective," of the incompetent.

Sixth, the prognosis with treatment must be examined. The likelihood of improvement or cure enhances the likelihood that an incompetent patient would accept treatment, but it is not conclusive.

Finally, the judge may review any other factors which appear relevant. After weighing the factors, the judge must reach a substituted judgment treatment decision. If the judge decides to order treatment with antipsychotic drugs for a committed incompetent patient, the judge should "authorize a treatment program which utilizes various specifically identified medications administered over a prolonged period of time. In such a case, the order should provide for periodic review to determine if the ward's condition, and circumstances have substantially changed." *Guardianship of Roe.* Once the decisions of incompetency and substituted judgment have been made, the burden shifts to the incompetent patient's guardian to seek modification of the order, should such modification be needed before the time for periodic review.

Medication to Prevent Immediate Harm

Questions 6 and 7. "Police power" and the use of antipsychotic drugs. The defendants assert that if they are unable to medicate, hospital administration becomes more difficult, lengths of stay increase, fewer patients can be treated, staff turnover increases and new personnel become more difficult to attract. The defendants also argue that the illness of one patient on a ward may be provocative, exacerbating the illness of other patients, and adversely affecting the doctors' ability to treat. In addition, they claim it is more difficult to conduct group therapy in an environment in which they cannot medicate with antipsychotic drugs. However, governmental interest "in permitting hospitals to care for those in their custody [is] not controlling, since a patient's right of self-determination [is] normally . . . superior to such institutional considerations." *Commissioner of Correction v. Myers.*

In *Guardianship of Roe*, we noted that "[c]ommentators and courts have identified abuses of antipsychotic medication by those claiming to act in an incompetent's best interests." In *Rogers*, the [district court] judge found that patients were involuntarily medicated with antipsychotic drugs over their objection in nonemergency situations. In *Davis v. Hubbard*, the judge found that seventy-three per cent of the patients of Lima (Ohio) State Hospital received psychotropic drugs, and that the high prescription rate "can be justified only for reasons other than treatment. . . namely, for the convenience of the staff and for punishment."

Nevertheless, psychiatric institutions must offer protection to third persons, whether staff members or patients, and must preserve security within the institution. However, when public safety and security are a consideration in the decision to administer antipsychotic drugs over a patient's objection, the "antipsychotic drugs function as chemical restraints forcibly imposed upon an unwilling individual who, if competent, would refuse such treatment." *Guardianship of Roe.* In such circumstances, the antipsychotic drug treatment is administered for the benefit of others, and the statutory and regulatory conditions for the use of chemical restraints must be followed.

[The law] requires that State mental health patients may be restrained "only in cases of emergency such as the occurrence of, or serious threat of, extreme violence, personal injury, or attempted suicide." In no case may chemical means of restraint be used without "written authorization . . . in advance by the superintendent or director of the I.C.U. [intensive care unit] or by a physician designated by him for this purpose." . . .

The use of chemicals to restrain State mental patients is limited to emergencies in which the patient harms, or threatens to harm, himself or others. We know of no reason why these rules regarding restraint should not be followed. The defendants suggest none. The statutes and regulations are clearly intended to set forth the exclusive means for use of chemical restraints, which include antipsychotic drugs. Use of the word "only" in [the law] means "for no other purpose." The statutory language permits the use of antipsychotic drugs as restraints only in specific, limited circumstances and does not allow expansion by doctors or courts.

We conclude that only if a patient poses an imminent threat of harm to himself or others, and only if there is no less intrusive alternative to antipsychotic drugs, may the Commonwealth invoke its police powers without prior court approval to treat the patient by forcible injection of antipsychotic drugs over the patient's objection. No other State interest is sufficiently compelling to warrant the extremely intrusive measures necessary for forcible medication with antipsychotic drugs. Any other result also would negate the Legislature's decision to regulate strictly the use of mind altering drugs as restraints.

Questions 8 and 9. Forcible antipsychotic medication essential to prevent "immediate, substantial, and irreversible deterioration of a serious mental illness." We have rejected the broad, traditional parens patriae power invoked by a State to do what is best for its citizens despite their own wishes, and instead have adopted the substituted judgment standard as the norm.

However, the State may, in rare circumstances, override a patient's refusal of medication under its so called "parens patriae" powers, even though no threat of violence exists. A patient may be treated against his will to prevent the "immediate, substantial, and irreversible deterioration of a serious mental illness," *Guardianship of Roe*, in cases in which "even the smallest of avoidable delays would be intolerable."

In such a situation, interim treatment may be given to an incompetent patient, or to one whom doctors, in the exercise of their professional judgment, believe to be incompetent. If a patient is medicated in order to avoid the "immediate, substantial, and irreversible deterioration of a serious mental illness," *Guardianship of Roe*, and the doctors determine that the antipsychotic medication should continue and the patient objects, the doctors must seek an adjudication of incompetence and if, after hearing, the patient is found to be incompetent, the judge should make a substituted judgment treatment plan determination.

"The Rogers case was marked through-out by a nihilistic attitude toward treatment."

Rogers Ignored Mentally Ill Patients' Incompetence to Determine Their Need for Treatment

Treatment Advocacy Center

The Treatment Advocacy Center is a national nonprofit organi-zation dedicated to eliminating barriers to the timely and effec-tive treatment of severe mental illnesses. It strongly favors the use of antipsychotic drugs. The following viewpoint expresses its view that the court decisions in Rogers v. Okin *and its subse-quent cases were biased against the use of medication and failed to take into account the belief of many psychiatrists that mental illness is in itself more mind-altering than the drugs used to treat it. In the opinion of the authors, the ruling has led to un-necessary costs and delays and has resulted in some patients not receiving treatment that they need. They state that involuntarily committed mental patients are never competent to make their own decisions about treatment and that they should be found incompetent by a judge at the time they are committed. The au-thors also advocate a mandatory second opinion by a psychia-trist in place of the judicial hearing on forcible medication of in-competent patients that the law in many states now requires.*

TreatmentAdvocacyCenter.org, "Rogers v. Okin," 1980. Copyright © 2008 Treatment Ad-vocacy Center. Reproduced by permission.

This class action suit, originally brought in 1975, grew out of organizing efforts by the Mental Patients Liberation Front at Boston State Hospital. Judi Chamberlin, a leader in the Front, has written that "many of the patients who became plaintiffs in the suit were members of a weekly patients' rights group at the hospital in which members of the Mental Patients Liberation Front met with interested patients." There were seven named plaintiffs—ranging in age from 52 to 20—who were hospitalized on two separate wards (the Austin and May units). The suit sought to enjoin the hospital, except in emergencies, from medicating them against their will or putting them in isolation. Most had a history of revolving door admissions: 38 year old Betty Bybel was admitted to the Austin Unit on 28 occasions between January 1973 and April 1975. Twenty-year-old Donna Hunt was first admitted at 15: falling ill with encephalitis at the age of three, she suffered organic brain damage. Fifty two year old Harold Warner had been held at Bridgewater State Hospital for the criminally insane for 17 years for assault and battery on a 12 year old girl. Rubie Rogers, by whose name the case came to be known, was in her late 30s, with a history of admissions and discharges beginning in 1965. For the four years previous to the suit she had been a voluntary patient at the hospital.

Greater Boston Legal Services (a legal services group financed by the federally funded Legal Services Corporation), which represented the patients, filed the case as a civil rights action (under Section 1983) and sought compensatory and punitive damages from members of the hospital staff.

The trial began in December 1977 and concluded at the end of January 1979, after 72 trial days involving more than 50 witnesses, 8,000 pages of transcripts plus 2,300 pages of post-trial briefs. Federal district court Judge Joseph Tauro handed down his decision in October 1979. The case, however, would not finally be resolved until November 29, 1983 (8 years from the time it was brought) after going on appeal to three additional courts (one of them twice).

The District Court's Ruling

At the trial level, Judge Tauro ruled that under Massachusetts law committed mental patients were presumed to be competent to manage their own affairs (dispose of property etc.), yet "such rights pale in comparison to the intimate decision as to whether to accept or refuse psychotropic medication." He asserted that in a non-emergency "it is an unreasonable invasion of privacy, and an affront to basic concepts of human dignity to permit the forced injection of mind altering drugs . . ." Although the state had a duty to make treatment available to mental patients, it had no duty to impose it on "the competent involuntary patient who prefers to refuse medication, regardless of its potential benefit."

In his opinion Judge Tauro took note of the defendant psychiatrists' argument that it was the state's parens patriae obligation to provide treatment for patients who had been committed for the purpose of treatment, even in the face of their opposition to it. He dismissed this argument on the grounds that "the State's interest in protecting the safety of the general public is the justification for commitment of mental patients." Involuntary treatment, Judge Tauro ruled, "is not necessary to protect the general public, since the patient has already been quarantined by commitment."

Judge Tauro accepted the argument that first amendment rights were at stake, which were contained in the brief of the plaintiffs' attorney, Richard Cole. "Realistically," Judge Tauro ruled, "the capacity to think and decide is a fundamental element of freedom," and whatever power the Constitution granted our government, "involuntary mind control is not one of them." And psychotropic drugs, he asserted, were "indisputably mind-altering."

The committed mental patient, said Judge Tauro, had the right to make treatment decisions until he was adjudicated incompetent by a judge. At this point, he noted, the parens patriae right of the state could be exercised and a guardian appointed by the court to make decisions, including treatment decisions, for the patient.

Judge Tauro did not grant the plaintiffs' claims for damages, however. He ruled that the staff had adhered to a generally accepted standard of care and could not know of a right to refuse treatment before it had been established by a court [his].

Later Rulings

Judge Tauro's decision was appealed, and while the Court of Appeals for the First Circuit (*Mills v. Rogers*) basically upheld the lower court, it expanded the definition of "emergency situation." Judge Tauro had defined an emergency as when "there is a substantial likelihood of . . . extreme violence, personal injury or attempted suicide." The Court of Appeals redefined emergency to include cases where the patient needed medication to prevent "further suffering of that patient or the rapid worsening of his clinical condition."

The Supreme Court granted certiorari [review by the Court] but then remanded the case back to the Court of Appeals in the light of *Roe*.[1] The Appellate Court asked the Massachusetts Supreme Judicial Court, which had decided *Roe*, for its opinion on the central issues in the case. The Massachusetts Supreme Judicial Court basically reiterated its position in *Roe*. That decision required that a court (not a guardian, as in Judge Tauro's decision) make the decision whether an incompetent patient should be treated, based on "substituted judgment," i.e., what the patient would have desired, were he com-

1. The Matter of Guardianship of Richard Roe III was decided by the Massachusetts Supreme Judicial Court in 1981. The court ruled that if a mentally ill patient who is incompetent to make treatment decisions refuses treatment, a court may only decide if treatment should continue based on what the patient would choose, if competent.

petent, taking into account he is not competent. Moreover, the substituted judgment decision required a full evidentiary hearing, with counsel for both sides, independent examiners and expert witnesses if requested.

The *Rogers* case initiated a model that would be copied by a number of other states, requiring court hearings before a patient may be medicated without his consent. This has imposed significant costs and delays in treatment, although the court in the end very rarely upholds the patient's refusal.

Problems Caused by the Court's Decision

The *Rogers* case was marked throughout by a nihilistic attitude toward treatment. The Mental Patients Liberation Front, which sparked the suit, denied there was such a thing as mental illness. Richard Cole, the legal services attorney who actually brought the suit, argued there was little value in treatment, since even those who supposedly "benefited" from it "continue to be unproductive," "a burden to their families," and "are as dependent and alienated as those confined to an institution." Judge Tauro looked on the drugs as impediments to freedom of thought (hence his assertion that they violated the First Amendment) without recognizing that mental illness was mind-altering, and the drugs mind-restorative. Both Judge Tauro and the Appeals Court emphasized the patient's right to freedom (the freedom to reject unwanted treatment) without recognizing the nature of mental illness—that psychosis was itself a prison and treatment could open the path to genuine autonomy.

The court gave the time-honored doctrine of parens patriae—the state's duty to intervene to help the helpless—short shrift. The state's interest only extended to "quarantining" the mentally ill who posed a danger to the public.

A number of studies have documented how obtaining so-called "Rogers orders" overruling patient refusals involves high monetary costs, delays, and shift of staff time from clinical care to paperwork. What goes undocumented are the numbers of seriously ill refusing patients who are quietly released to the streets and shelters. Nor does the wasteful and unwieldy system even work as intended. Judges are supposed to determine if the refusing patient is competent and then be guided by the principle of "substituted judgment" in deciding if the incompetent patient is to be treated. But mental health law expert Alexander Brooks has pointed out that the various courts that issued opinions in the *Rogers* case never explained what evidence judges should look for to determine if a patient was incompetent. Without guidance on this crucial matter, judges, studies have shown, in practice primarily focus on how "dangerous" the patient is, to him or others. And then in practically all cases, they forget about "substituted judgment" and simply order treatment.

The *Rogers* model ignored a much more sensible way of allowing patient protests to be considered—the mandatory second psychiatric opinion instituted by the *Rennie [v. Klein]* case in New Jersey.

For states that have a adopted a *Rogers* model, a simple reform offers the best solution to the manifold problems that model has caused—namely, to require the judge to evaluate the patient's capacity to make his own treatment decisions at the same time he commits him. Utah's mental health statutes require that a judge find a patient incompetent to make his own treatment decisions as a precondition for commitment.

This ideally should be the law in all states and becomes a necessary reform in all states that have adopted a *Rogers* model.

It must be remembered that the patient's assumed "competence," which is the basis for the right to refuse, is a legal fiction, originally intended to facilitate treatment. Up until the 1960s, commitment to a mental hospital in most states automatically stripped the individual of all his civil rights. In U.S. Senate hearings in 1961 it was argued that the mentally ill and their families were reluctant to seek treatment early because of the legal consequences that could haunt them later. Certainly it was a wise reform to ensure that mentally ill individuals kept their civil rights. But the individual who is committed is clearly incompetent to make his own decisions respecting his need for treatment—if he understood his need for treatment why would he need to be involuntarily committed? Finding him incompetent in this regard is thus a logical precondition for commitment, and this needs to be established by law.

*"She was willing to put herself on the
line and fight for her rights and fight
for the rights of other people who were
in her situation."*

Rubie Rogers Helped
Win Key Rights for Patients
with Mental Illness

Bryan Marquard

Bryan Marquard is a staff writer for the Boston Globe. *In this
article, written at the time of Rubie Rogers's death in 2009, he
says that as the chief plaintiff in* Rogers v. Okin, *she helped to
determine the course states took in establishing key rights for the
mentally ill. In Massachusetts, where the case was filed, the mentally ill must now give informed consent before being given
medication, and those who are legally incompetent to do so are
entitled to a judicial procedure known as a "Rogers hearing."
Marqaurd quotes from Rubie Rogers's testimony at the original
trial of the case, in which she described the terrible effects forced
drugging had on her, as well as statements from the ruling of the
district court judge. Many psychiatrists disagree with that ruling,
he states. He also tells something about Rogers's life both before
and after the trial and about the Ruby Rogers Center in Massachusetts, which assists people who have been patients in the
mental health system.*

Bryan Marquard, "Ruby Rogers Helped Win Key Rights for Mentally Ill," *Boston Globe*,
February 20, 2009. Copyright © 2009 Globe Newspaper Company. Reproduced by permission.

In Turners Falls [Massachusetts], nearly 100 miles west of where she spent decades confined in Boston psychiatric facilities, Ruby Rogers died quietly in a nursing home, a relatively anonymous end for a woman whose name is routinely invoked during Massachusetts court hearings involving the mentally ill.

"They said she just lay down and went to sleep," said her sister, Claudette Smith of Dorchester.

Ms. Rogers, who spent her last years at the Farren Care Center, left a sweeping legacy that established key rights for the mentally ill in the Commonwealth. With *Rogers v. Okin*, the landmark case that bore her name, she also helped determine the course other states took to help certain psychiatric patients participate in decisions about their treatment. Courts and lawmakers elsewhere examined the precedent that Ms. Rogers and six others set with the lawsuit they filed in 1975.

As a result of that case, the mentally ill in Massachusetts must give informed consent before doctors and nurses administer medication. A doctor who believes a patient isn't competent to grant permission must schedule what is known as a "Rogers hearing." If the patient is found to be legally incompetent, a judge—through what is called "substituted judgment"—decides whether the patient would want to accept the prescribed treatment.

The state Department of Mental Health plans to honor Ms. Rogers, who was 71 when she died Jan. 12 [2009], during a legislative breakfast March 2 at the State House.

The case began when Richard W. Cole, only months out of law school and working for Greater Boston Legal Services, went to Boston State Hospital as an advocate for the patients and listened to their complaints. At the time, mentally ill patients could not refuse treatment in Massachusetts once they were committed to a facility such as Boston State.

Among the seven patients who took part in the court fight, he said, Ms. Rogers was notable, in part because she had voluntarily entered the hospital seeking help.

"Ruby became the lead plaintiff," Cole said. "We decided that based on Ruby's personality, her strength, how vibrant she was as a woman, and also because of her story, that she made the most sense to be the first name in the litigation."

Harrowing Tales

Taking the stand in US District Court in 1978, Ms. Rogers told harrowing tales. Even though her concerns about her mental stability prompted her to seek treatment, she ended up setting her hair on fire in an attempt to get transferred out of Boston State Hospital after she was repeatedly forced to take antipsychotic medications with devastating side effects.

"It felt like something was crawling on my feet and biting them," she testified. "I didn't sleep . . . my arms and legs were jerking, twitching uncontrollably . . . my whole body quivered. When I would put on my clothes, it would take about an hour to put my slacks on. I couldn't put my hands up to comb my hair."

Ms. Rogers testified that if she refused to take her medicine, "I was just seized by six or seven men and rushed into seclusion and given the needle." Locked in the seclusion room with no toilet, she "had to go on the floor," which was cleaned only when a nurse came by to hand out medication.

"You always felt you were smothering or dying," she said of being confined in the room. "It felt like it was 475 degrees in there. I couldn't breathe. Most of the time I couldn't get water. I used to holler to get out."

In October 1979, Judge Joseph L. Tauro issued a stern ruling in the case, which was appealed to the US Supreme Court before being sent back to state courts for adjudication.

"Whatever powers the Constitution has granted our government, involuntary mind control is not one of them, absent extraordinary circumstances," Tauro wrote. "The fact that mind control takes place in a mental institution in the form of medically sound treatment of mental disease is not, itself, an extraordinary circumstance warranting an unsanctioned intrusion on the integrity of a human being."

In a nod toward Ms. Rogers, he ruled that voluntary patients had the same right to refuse treatment as those committed involuntarily. And addressing issues she and others raised in testimony, Tauro wrote that "it is an unreasonable invasion of privacy, and an affront to basic concepts of human dignity, to permit forced injection of a mind-altering drug into the buttocks of a competent patient unwilling to give informed consent."

Opposition from Psychiatrists

Then and now, many psychiatrists disagreed with the ruling.

"I think it built into the law that families cannot be trusted to make decisions for their children or parents or spouses," said Alan A. Stone, the Touroff-Glueck professor of law and psychiatry at Harvard University. "In my view, judges have no basis to make these decisions. They don't know the patients, they don't know the illnesses, and they don't know the families. So we go through long, complicated hearings about whether patients should receive medications for their psychoses."

Born in Clinchco, a tiny rural town in western Virginia, Ruby Rogers moved to Boston after high school and encouraged her younger siblings to follow. "There was no work in Virginia for young girls or people of color, and she came here to better herself," her sister said.

Ms. Rogers worked as a nurse's aide at Boston City Hospital before deciding she needed help for mental illness. By then, she had six children, who went into foster care when Ms. Rogers was hospitalized, her sister said. Smith said the family has not been able to locate them.

"She loved her children dearly," Smith said. "Before she died, that's all she talked about."

In addition to Smith, Ms. Rogers leaves two brothers, Robert of Hyde Park and Jessie Anderson of Mattapan; and three other sisters, Kay Tyree of Sharon, Nancy Blackley of Walpole, and Brenda Ellis of Norton, Va.

"Ruby was a beautiful person, and I miss her," Smith said. "I'm going to take her remains to Virginia and bury her next to our mother, sometime in the spring."

Ms. Rogers remains a presence in Massachusetts courts and in Somerville, where the Ruby Rogers Center assists those who have been patients in the mental health system.

"She was willing to put herself on the line and fight for her rights and fight for the rights of other people who were in her situation," said Judi Chamberlain of Arlington, an advocate who formerly was program coordinator at the center.

"For all those years, Ruby hung in there, never wavered, and was a great spokesperson for what was really the core issue of the case," said Cole, her attorney. "This really helped her as she struggled with her problems over the years, the knowledge that she had accomplished something real and important."

CHAPTER 3

Defining the Rights of Institutionalized Patients

Case Overview

Youngberg v. Romeo (1982)

Nicholas Romeo was severely retarded; although an adult, he had the mental capacity of an eighteen-month-old child. He could not talk and lacked basic self-care skills. He lived with his parents until he was in his late twenties, but after his father died, his mother was unable to care for him or control his violence, so she had him committed to the Pennhurst State School and Hospital in Pennsylvania.

At Pennhurst, Romeo was often injured by his own violence as well as in encounters with other residents who were reacting to him. His mother was concerned about these injuries and repeatedly objected to the way he was treated. Finally, she filed suit against Pennhurst. The complaint alleged that its officials knew, or should have known, about the frequent injuries and that they failed to take any preventive action, thus violating Romeo's rights under the Eighth and Fourteenth Amendments.

While the suit was pending, Romeo was transferred from his ward to the hospital for treatment of a broken arm. In the infirmary he was physically restrained in order to protect him and other patients. After this, an amended complaint was filed alleging that the defendants were restraining him for prolonged periods on a routine basis. This second complaint also added a claim for monetary compensation to Romeo for the defendants' failure to provide him with appropriate "treatment or programs for his mental retardation."

An eight-day jury trial was held in April 1978. At its close the court instructed the jury that "if any or all of the defendants were aware of and failed to take all reasonable steps to prevent repeated attacks upon Romeo," such failure deprived him of constitutional rights. The jury also was instructed that if the defendants shackled Romeo or denied him treatment "as a punishment for filing this lawsuit," his constitutional rights were violated under the Eighth Amendment. Finally, the jury was instructed that only if they found the defendants "deliberate[ly] indifferen[t] to the serious medical [and psychological] needs" of Romeo could they conclude that his Eighth and Fourteenth Amendment rights had been violated. The jury returned a verdict in favor of the Pennhurst officials.

The court of appeals reversed this ruling and remanded the case for a new trial. It found that under the Fourteenth Amendment, mentally disabled individuals retain liberty interests in freedom of movement and in personal security. The appellate court said that these interests are "fundamental liberties" that can be limited only by an "overriding, nonpunitive" state interest. It further found that involuntarily committed patients have a liberty interest in habilitation designed to treat their mental retardation. The judges did not agree, however, on the standard to be used in determining whether a patient's rights had been violated.

The Supreme Court, in a landmark decision, agreed that mentally disabled individuals have the constitutional right to reasonably safe conditions of confinement, freedom from unreasonable bodily restraints, and such minimally adequate training as reasonably may be required by these interests. Whether Nicholas Romeo's constitutional rights had been violated must be determined by balancing these liberty interests against the relevant state interests, it said. And, significantly, it held that the proper standard for determining if the state had adequately protected such rights was whether professional judgment had been exercised. It asserted that judgment exercised by a qualified professional must be presumed valid.

"*[The state] may not restrain residents [of mental institutions] except when and to the extent professional judgment deems this necessary to assure such safety or to provide needed training.*"

The Court's Decision: Patients with Mental Illness Have a Right to Training and Freedom from Bodily Restraints

Lewis Powell

Lewis Powell was a justice of the U.S. Supreme Court from 1972 to 1987. He was known as a judicial moderate. In the following majority opinion he wrote in the landmark case Youngberg v. Romeo, *he rules that involuntarily committed mentally retarded persons have rights of which commitment does not deprive them, including the right to safe conditions and the right to freedom from bodily restraint. He then considers the issue of training, which is less clear-cut, and concludes that some training may be necessary to avoid unconstitutional infringement of these rights. Finally, he states that courts must defer to the judgment of professionals in determining what training is reasonable, as judges and juries are no better qualified to make such decisions, and that interference by the judiciary with the internal operation of mental institutions should be minimized.*

Lewis Powell, majority opinion, *Duane Youngberg, etc., et al. v. Nicholas Romeo*, U.S. Supreme Court, June 18, 1982.

We consider here for the first time the substantive rights of involuntarily committed mentally retarded persons under the Fourteenth Amendment to the Constitution. In this case, respondent [Nicholas Romeo] has been committed under the laws of Pennsylvania, and he does not challenge the commitment. Rather, he argues that he has a constitutionally protected liberty interest in safety, freedom of movement, and training within the institution; and that petitioners infringed these rights by failing to provide constitutionally required conditions of confinement.

The mere fact that Romeo has been committed under proper procedures does not deprive him of all substantive liberty interests under the Fourteenth Amendment. Indeed, the state concedes that respondent has a right to adequate food, shelter, clothing, and medical care. We must decide whether liberty interests also exist in safety, freedom of movement, and training. If such interests do exist, we must further decide whether they have been infringed in this case.

Respondent's first two claims involve liberty interests recognized by prior decisions of this Court, interests that involuntary commitment proceedings do not extinguish. The first is a claim to safe conditions. In the past, this Court has noted that the right to personal security constitutes a "historic liberty interest" protected substantively by the Due Process Clause. And that right is not extinguished by lawful confinement, even for penal purposes. If it is cruel and unusual punishment to hold convicted criminals in unsafe conditions, it must be unconstitutional to confine the involuntarily committed—who may not be punished at all—in unsafe conditions.

Next, respondent claims a right to freedom from bodily restraint. In other contexts, the existence of such an interest is clear in the prior decisions of this Court. Indeed, "[l]iberty from bodily restraint always has been recognized as the core of the liberty protected by the Due Process Clause from arbitrary governmental action." *Greenholtz v. Nebraska Penal In-*

mates. This interest survives criminal conviction and incarceration. Similarly, it must also survive involuntary commitment.

The Right to Training

Respondent's remaining claim is more troubling. In his words, he asserts a "constitutional right to minimally adequate habilitation." This is a substantive due process claim that is said to be grounded in the liberty component of the Due Process Clause of the Fourteenth Amendment. The term "habilitation," used in psychiatry, is not defined precisely or consistently in the opinions below or in the briefs of the parties or the *amici* [friends of the court]. The term refers to "training and development of needed skills." Respondent emphasizes that the right he asserts is for "minimal" training, and he would leave the type and extent of training to be determined on a case-by-case basis "in light of present medical or other scientific knowledge."

In addressing the asserted right to training, we start from established principles. As a general matter, a State is under no constitutional duty to provide substantive services for those within its border. When a person is institutionalized—and wholly dependent on the State—it is conceded by petitioners that a duty to provide certain services and care does exist, although even then a State necessarily has considerable discretion in determining the nature and scope of its responsibilities. Nor must a State "choose between attacking every aspect of a problem or not attacking the problem at all." *Dandridge v. Williams.*

Respondent, in light of the severe character of his retardation, concedes that no amount of training will make possible his release. And he does not argue that if he were still at home, the State would have an obligation to provide training at its expense. The record reveals that respondent's primary needs are bodily safety and a minimum of physical restraint,

111

and respondent clearly claims training related to these needs. As we have recognized that there is a constitutionally protected liberty interest in safety and freedom from restraint, training may be necessary to avoid unconstitutional infringement of those rights. On the basis of the record before us, it is quite uncertain whether respondent seeks any "habilitation" or training unrelated to safety and freedom from bodily restraints. In his brief to this Court, Romeo indicates that even the self-care programs he seeks are needed to reduce his aggressive behavior. And in his offer of proof to the trial court, respondent repeatedly indicated that, if allowed to testify, his experts would show that additional training programs, including self-care programs, were needed to reduce his aggressive behavior. If, as seems the case, respondent seeks only training related to safety and freedom from restraints, this case does not present the difficult question whether a mentally retarded person, involuntarily committed to a state institution, has some general constitutional right to training *per se*, even when no type or amount of training would lead to freedom.

Chief Judge Seitz, in language apparently adopted by respondent, observed: "I believe that the plaintiff has a constitutional right to minimally adequate care and treatment. The existence of a constitutional right to care and treatment is no longer a novel legal proposition."

Chief Judge Seitz did not identify or otherwise define— beyond the right to reasonable safety and freedom from physical restraint the "minimally adequate care and treatment" that appropriately may be required for this respondent. In the circumstances presented by this case, and on the basis of the record developed to date, we agree with his view and conclude that respondent's liberty interests require the State to provide minimally adequate or reasonable training to ensure safety and freedom from undue restraint. In view of the kinds of treatment sought by respondent and the evidence of record, we need go no further in this case.

Conflict Between Safety and Freedom from Restraint

We have established that Romeo retains liberty interests in safety and freedom from bodily restraint. Yet these interests are not absolute; indeed to some extent they are in conflict. In operating an institution such as Pennhurst, there are occasions in which it is necessary for the State to restrain the movement of residents—for example, to protect them as well as others from violence. Similar restraints may also be appropriate in a training program. And an institution cannot protect its residents from all danger of violence if it is to permit them to have any freedom of movement. The question then is not simply whether a liberty interest has been infringed but whether the extent or nature of the restraint or lack of absolute safety is such as to violate due process.

In determining whether a substantive right protected by the Due Process Clause has been violated, it is necessary to balance "the liberty of the individual" and "the demands of an organized society." *Poe v. Ullman.* In seeking this balance in other cases, the Court has weighed the individual's interest in liberty against the State's asserted reasons for restraining individual liberty, for example, we considered a challenge to pre-trial detainees' confinement conditions. We agreed that the detainees, not yet convicted of the crime charged, could not be punished. But we upheld those restrictions on liberty that were reasonably related to legitimate government objectives and not tantamount to punishment. We have taken a similar approach in deciding procedural due process challenges to civil commitment proceedings. For example, we considered a challenge to state procedures for commitment of a minor with parental consent. In determining that *procedural* due process did not mandate an adversarial hearing, we weighed the liberty interest of the individual against the legitimate interests of the State, including the fiscal and administrative burdens additional procedures would entail.

113

Accordingly, whether respondent's constitutional rights have been violated must be determined by balancing his liberty interests against the relevant state interests. If there is to be any uniformity in protecting these interests, this balancing cannot be left to the unguided discretion of a judge or jury. We therefore turn to consider the proper standard for determining whether a State adequately has protected the rights of the involuntarily committed mentally retarded.

We think the standard articulated by Chief Judge Seitz affords the necessary guidance and reflects the proper balance between the legitimate interests of the State and the rights of the involuntarily committed to reasonable conditions of safety and freedom from unreasonable restraints. He would have held that "the Constitution only requires that the courts make certain that professional judgment in fact was exercised. It is not appropriate for the courts to specify which of several professionally acceptable choices should have been made." Persons who have been involuntarily committed are entitled to more considerate treatment and conditions of confinement than criminals whose conditions of confinement are designed to punish. At the same time, this standard is lower than the "compelling" or "substantial" necessity tests the Court of Appeals would require a State to meet to justify use of restraints or conditions of less than absolute safety. We think this requirement would place an undue burden on the administration of institutions such as Pennhurst and also would restrict unnecessarily the exercise of professional judgment as to the needs of residents.

Validity of Decisions Made by Professionals

Moreover, we agree that respondent is entitled to minimally adequate training. In this case, the minimally adequate training required by the Constitution is such training as may be reasonable in light of respondent's liberty interests in safety and freedom from unreasonable restraints. In determining what is "reasonable" in this and in any case presenting a claim for training by a State we emphasize that courts must show deference to the judgment exercised by a qualified professional. By so limiting judicial review of challenges to conditions in state institutions, interference by the federal judiciary with the internal operations of these institutions should be minimized. Moreover, there certainly is no reason to think judges or juries are better qualified than appropriate professionals in making such decisions. For these reasons, the decision, if made by a professional, is presumptively valid; liability may be imposed only when the decision by the professional is such a substantial departure from accepted professional judgment, practice, or standards as to demonstrate that the person responsible actually did not base the decision on such a judgment. In an action for damages against a professional in his individual capacity, however, the professional will not be liable if he was unable to satisfy his normal professional standards because of budgetary constraints; in such a situation, good-faith immunity would bar liability.

In deciding this case, we have weighed those postcommitment interests cognizable as liberty interests under the Due Process Clause of the Fourteenth Amendment against legitimate state interests and in light of the constraints under which most state institutions necessarily operate. We repeat that the State concedes a duty to provide adequate food, shelter, clothing, and medical care. These are the essentials of the care that the State must provide. The State also has the unquestioned duty to provide reasonable safety for all residents and personnel within the institution. And it may not restrain residents except when and to the extent professional judgment deems this necessary to assure such safety or to provide needed training. In this case, therefore, the State is under a duty to provide respondent with such training as an appropriate professional would consider reasonable to ensure his safety and to facilitate his ability to function free from bodily restraints. It may well be unreasonable not to provide training when training could significantly reduce the need for restraints or the likelihood of violence.

Respondent thus enjoys constitutionally protected interests in conditions of reasonable care and safety, reasonably nonrestrictive confinement conditions, and such training as may be required by these interests. Such conditions of confinement would comport fully with the purpose of respondent's commitment. In determining whether the State has met its obligations in these respects, decisions made by the appropriate professional are entitled to a presumption of correctness. Such a presumption is necessary to enable institutions of this type— often, unfortunately, overcrowded and understaffed—to continue to function. A single professional may have to make decisions with respect to a number of residents with widely varying needs and problems in the course of a normal day. The administrators, and particularly professional personnel, should not be required to make each decision in the shadow of an action for damages.

> *"The decision is a cornerstone in what has become a 'patients' rights' movement comparable in many respects to the prisoners' and defendants' rights thrust."*

Youngberg v. Romeo Is a Cornerstone of the Patients' Rights Movement

Fred Barbash

Fred Barbash was a staff writer for the Washington Post. *In the following news report on the Supreme Court's decision in* Youngberg v. Romeo, *he describes the decision and states that although it leaves many questions unanswered, it is a cornerstone of the patients' rights movement. He points out that Justice Lewis Powell said patients should have at least the constitutional protections afforded prisoners, such as a right to safe conditions and a right to be free of unnecessary physical restraints, plus as much training as is needed to enable them to function safely in the hospital. Mental health experts consider the ruling an important change in the law, says Barbash, because for the first time the Court said mental institutions have to do more for patients than basic maintenance.*

The Supreme Court yesterday [June 18, 1982] for the first time established constitutional rights for people committed to institutions for the mentally retarded, including unprecedented, but limited, guarantees of a minimum level of training.

Fred Barbash, "High Court Establishes Rights for Retarded in Institutions," *Washington Post*, June 19, 1982. Copyright © 1982, The Washington Post. Reprinted with permission.

The court also said institutions have an obligation, enforceable in the courts, to provide a reasonable amount of physical freedom as well as safety for involuntarily committed patients.

At the same time, Justice Lewis F. Powell Jr., writing for the 8-to-1 majority, cautioned judges to respect the professional judgments and budgetary restraints of the institutions and not require them to "make each decision in the shadow" of possible lawsuits.

The opinion, carefully balancing the competing interests in one of the most publicized cases of the current term, applies directly to hospitals for the mentally retarded but also is expected to affect mental hospitals. There are an estimated 150,000 people in state institutions for the mentally retarded.

"Persons who have been involuntarily committed are entitled to more considerate treatment and conditions of confinement than criminals whose conditions of confinement are designed to punish," Powell said.

The decision left many questions unanswered, such as what constitutes reasonable freedom, and many points unclear, in an apparent attempt to allow flexibility for professional judgments. It also allowed numerous defenses for hospital officials sued for mistreatment, including a defense that the problems were caused by "budgetary restraints."

Nevertheless, the decision is a cornerstone in what has become a "patients' rights" movement comparable in many respects to the prisoners' and defendants' rights thrust of the '60s and '70s. Nearly all the states face litigation in this field.

Twenty-one, fearing federal judges would soon begin looking excessively over their shoulders, asked the Supreme Court to resolve the issues, preserving to the extent possible maximum flexibility for their state institutions.

Yesterday's case began with a suit brought on behalf of Nicholas Romeo, 33, a man with the mental capacity of an 18-month-old child. Romeo's mother had him legally committed in May, 1974, to the Pennhurst State School and Hospital near Philadelphia. That state-run institution has been the subject of numerous suits and complaints of mistreatment.

She became concerned about her son's treatment after learning that he had been injured at least 70 times both by his own hand and by others reacting to his aggressive behavior. She also learned that officials had repeatedly confined him in physical arm restraints during portions of each day.

She sued the officials for damages under federal civil rights laws, seeking broad constitutional guarantees for patients to be free of physical restraints, and guaranteed rights to comprehensive training and development programs.

She lost at trial, but the 3rd U.S. Circuit Court of Appeals, in a divided ruling, ordered a new trial because of misinterpretations of constitutional law by the District Court.

Pennhurst appealed, but yesterday the Supreme Court agreed with the appeals court and issued its own guidelines for these cases. The justices agreed unanimously that the case should be returned to the lower court for a new trial.

Chief Justice Warren E. Burger agreed with much of the ruling, but dissented from any right to treatment.

The Rights of Patients

Powell said that the patients should have at least the constitutional protections afforded prisoners, such as a right to safe conditions and the right to be free from unnecessary physical restraints. He noted that unlike prison inmates, the patients at issue in yesterday's case "may not be punished at all."

The right to treatment is a more difficult problem, Powell said, because the Constitution guarantees no substantive services to anyone. He said the least that could be demanded, however, was that the involuntarily committed receive the training they need to function safely in the hospital, without hurting themselves or others. This would also help them avoid the need for shackling and physical confinement.

Powell based his ruling on the due process clause of the 14th Amendment, which protects the personal physical liberty of individuals from unfair or unreasonable incursions by the states. The question, he said, was how to determine what is fair in this situation.

". . . In determining what is reasonable," he said, "we emphasize that courts must show deference to the judgment exercised by a qualified professional. By so limiting judicial review of challenges to conditions in state institutions, interference by the federal judiciary with the internal operations of these institutions should be minimized. Moreover, there certainly is no reason to think judges or juries are better qualified than appropriate professionals in making such decisions."

The decisions of the professionals should be considered generally valid by the courts, Powell said, unless there is "such a substantial departure from accepted professional judgment, practice or standards as to demonstrate that the person responsible actually did not base the decision on such a judgment."

Experts in mental health law said yesterday that even with its ambiguities, the ruling in *Youngberg v. Romeo* was an important change in the law.

"It is a positive step in the right direction," said Norman S. Rosenberg, director of the Mental Health Law Project. Rosenberg said it was the first time the court had said that such institutions have to do anything besides basic maintenance for patients, the first time any "affirmative right" to training had been granted. Joel Klein, who filed a friend of the court brief for the American Psychiatric Association expressing concern about maintaining professional autonomy for hospital officials, said he felt that need had been satisfied.

"In Youngberg v. Romeo . . . *the Supreme Court transformed the roles of mental health professionals from secondary players to the principal decisionmakers regarding what constitutes the minimum treatment a state must provide to those in its care."*

Youngberg Enlarged the Role of Mental Health Professionals in Institutional Reform

Mark A. Small and Randy K. Otto

Mark A. Small is a professor of psychology at the Institute on Family and Neighborhood Life at Clemson University. He is also a licensed attorney. Randy K. Otto is an associate professor of psychology at the Florida Mental Health Institute at the University of South Florida. In the following viewpoint they explain that the Supreme Court's decision in Youngberg v. Romeo *dramatically changed efforts to improve mental health care for children. Previously, mental health professionals participated in court cases involving reform only as expert witnesses, but in its* Youngberg *ruling the Court said the judges should defer to the judgment of professionals. It said that their decisions must be respected as long as they were in accord with accepted practice in their fields. Therefore, professionals can now recommend services that are presently unavailable, although they cannot simply ignore the cost of these services. Also, they can work to raise current professional standards for conditions at mental institutions.*

Mark A. Small and Randy K. Otto, "Utilizing the 'Professional Judgment Standard' in Child Advocacy," *Journal of Clinical Child Psychology*, March 1991. Reproduced by permission of Taylor & Francis Group, LLC, www.taylorandfrancis.com.

Mental health professionals working in state institutions have the potential to play an important role in child advocacy efforts. Because a significant number of children are treated in institutions, legal advocacy efforts aimed at improving the care and treatment in institutions may properly be regarded as child advocacy efforts. Indeed, litigation aimed at reforming conditions in institutions frequently involves children as plaintiffs. Although there is some debate about the efficacy of such efforts, mental health professionals are in a new and precarious position in the wake of institutional services litigation. There are now novel tactics mental health professionals can employ to increase the availability of appropriate services for children, although at this point, the tacks remain largely untested.

Given the current legal context in which treatment decisions are made, there are two potential strategies professionals may utilize to increase mental health and related services to children. One involves exercising a professional judgment (making a treatment decision) ordering services that may be currently unavailable. This strategy essentially advocates for change at an individual level, altering the specific services an individual receives. A second strategy is to raise current professional standards regarding the conditions at institutions. This strategy targets change at an institutional level by raising the minimum requirements of living conditions and treatment services in institutions. . . .

Youngberg v. Romeo

The focal point of institutional reform advocacy efforts changed dramatically with the Supreme Court's decision in *Youngberg v. Romeo* (1982). Prior to *Youngberg*, advocates interested in improving conditions in institutions frequently argued for a federal constitutional "right to treatment" for institutional residents, or at least, placement in the "least restrictive alternative." Additional reform strategies included preventing institutionalization of children and closing down institutions.

Mental health professionals in these institutional reform cases typically participated as expert witnesses. The mental health professional might testify about the conditions in a particular institution and compare them to the conditions that might ideally exist in the institution. In *Youngberg v. Romeo*, however, the Supreme Court transformed the roles of mental health professionals from secondary players to the principal decisionmakers regarding what constitutes the minimum treatment a state must provide to those in its care. Although the doctrine of judicial deference to professional judgment existed prior to Youngberg it was in Youngberg that the Supreme Court's hands off approach to potential involvement in mental health administration gained significant favor.

The Court first ruled that involuntarily committed retarded people have rights under the due process clause of the Fourteenth Amendment that include safety, freedom from undue restraint, and the "minimally adequate or reasonable training" necessary to ensure these liberty interests. Whether these rights have been violated must be resolved by balancing the individual's liberty interests against the state's interests.

Rather than charge judges and juries with the task of balancing these interests in each case, the Court held that the decision should be made by professionals. According to the Court, a professional decisionmaker means "a person who is competent, whether by education, training or experience, to make a particular decision at issue." Specifically, treatment decisions were to be made by "persons with degrees in medicine or nursing or with appropriate training in areas such as psychology, physical therapy or the care and training of the retarded."

The Supreme Court ruled that in cases where the adequacy of treatment was an issue, courts must defer to professional judgment. In other words, professional judgment is presumptively valid. In articulating a specific standard of liability, the Court gave wide latitude to professionals making treatment decisions. Concerning the standard of liability, the Court ruled:

> liability may be imposed only when the decision by the professional is such a substantial departure from accepted professional judgment, practice, or standards as to demonstrate that the person responsible actually did not base the decision on such a judgment. In an action for damages against a professional in his individual capacity, however, the professional will not be liable if he was unable to satisfy his normal professional standards because of budgetary constraints; in such a situation, good-faith immunity would bar liability.

This rule makes the standard of liability one of almost gross negligence. As long as the professional makes a decision within the broad boundaries of accepted practice, there will be no liability. The professional judgment standard and the corresponding rule for liability is considered by some to discourage judicial interference with the mental health system.

Standards of Liability

To determine whether a mental health professional's conduct falls below acceptable standards, courts first identify what acceptable practice is through the use of experts from the field of concern. Mental health professionals working in institutions are expected to adhere to the standard of care demonstrated by reasonably prudent specialists in their discipline. The standard of care that is due may be shaped by professional standards (e.g., ethical codes, specialty guidelines) as well as prior legal decisions. Although there have been some cases in which courts have ruled that standard professional practice was inadequate and imposed liability, the courts generally defer to standards established by the particular profession.

Traditionally, courts used the locality rule, which required that the professional only exercise the care and skill common to professionals in the same or similar locale. With increased specialization, however, the locality rule has given way so that a national standard of care is now defined for many professions and specialties.

Defining a standard of care for the mental health professions, however, presents a unique challenge. As compared to other health professions and specialties, it is more difficult to achieve agreement regarding what types of treatment are indicated in what types of situations. This is probably a function of the limited knowledge base regarding the etiology and treatment of mental disorders and the large number of schools of therapy.

These factors work together so that even if a standard of care can be established, it is likely that the professional will be given considerable latitude. Accordingly, as evidenced by the low rate of malpractice suits against mental health professionals, findings of liability are unlikely. Because it is difficult to prove that treatment decisions will fall outside the general practice, other strategies must be developed for institutional reform.

Advocacy for Improving Individual Services

After the Supreme Court's decision in *Youngberg*, one strategy seemed obvious for advocating for changes in services. Qualified mental health professionals could simply determine that some treatment was necessary for an individual and the state would be required to provide it. However, litigation ensued when states did not offer the services recommended by qualified professionals or could not afford to provide them. Three circuit courts deciding such issues generally held that a state was not obligated to provide such services. However, in two reported cases (both initially involving children from the third and fourth circuits), courts ordered that the services recommended by a professional be provided, even though they were currently unavailable.

In *Clark v. Cohen* (1985), a federal district court found that substantive due process rights were implicated in the case of a 44-year-old mildly mentally retarded woman who resided at a state institution for the mentally retarded since her commitment at the age of 15. All the institution's professional staff agreed that the plaintiff (Clark) should be placed in a community living arrangement (CLA) which was not available due to a shortage of funds. Accordingly, she filed suit seeking injunctive relief in the form of her transfer to a CLA.

Noting that professional opinion was unanimous that Clark should be transferred to a CLA, the federal district court ruled that her substantive rights under *Youngberg* had been violated. Consequently, the state released Clark and provided programs and services, as ordered by the court. This finding was upheld on appeal and remedial measures were considered proper "to undo the harmful effects of past constitutional violations."

The federal district court rejected the state's argument that institutional placement should be allowed whenever there are insufficient funds or resources available for nonresidential services. The court emphasized, however, that its decision did not establish a right to a CLA. The court also held that Clark should not be placed in an institutional setting unless a community placement could not be developed and ordered the defendants to provide a CLA. Unavailability of funding was considered irrelevant to whether a placement could be developed. Thus, the court interpreted the *Youngberg* professional judgment standard to mean that a treatment decision "has to be one based on medical or psychological criteria and not on exigency, administrative convenience, or other non-medical criteria." The court found that the treatment decisions had been ignored "for reasons unrelated to professional assessments of plaintiff's needs" and ordered community placement.

The *Youngberg* holding is considered by many to inhibit reform, because it defaults to the status quo. The institutional professional who recommends and offers treatment that is a substantial departure from accepted practice is only subject to a court ordering more intensive (and costly) treatment. Liability will only be found in the most outrageous cases.

Although this is true, Clark demonstrated that the holding is most accurately depicted as a double-edged sword. The courts' deference to professional judgment in establishing constitutionally required institutional services suggests that the availability of more and better services can be accomplished by making treatment recommendations that do not consider only currently available treatments. When professional judgments/treatment recommendations are made in the institutional setting and they are not followed, reform advocates may use these (unfollowed) recommendations and judgments as grounds for establishing what is constitutionally required of the state. To the degree that they make treatment recommendations based on clients' needs rather than on simply what is available, mental health professionals working in institutions may facilitate change. As suggested in *Thomas S. v. Morrow* (1984), however, institutional professionals cannot simply ignore cost factors when making treatment recommendations.

In *Thomas S.* a district court concluded that the treatment that was provided to the plaintiff was not consistent with the treatment recommendations of the professionals who initially evaluated him. The court assumed that differences between the treatment provided for Thomas and that recommended by the hospital treatment team were due to modification of the professionals' judgment "to conform to the *available* treatment rather than to the *appropriate* treatment" for Thomas's condition.

The court refused to consider the funding problems or lack of available alternative treatments. . . . Concluding that Thomas was "entitled to treatment recommended by qualified professionals whose judgment is unsullied by consideration of the fact that the state does not now provide appropriate treatment or funding for appropriate treatment," the court required Thomas's guardian and the state to develop a treatment plan and furnish the professionally recommended treatment, including placement in a community residential program. In affirming the decision on appeal, the appellate court found no evidence that the evaluation team did not consider costs when prescribing Thomas's treatment, and refused to assume that the professionals drafted prohibitively expensive recommendations. . . .

Both cases illustrate how mental health treatment decisions can be used to provide services that would not be provided otherwise. . . . Both cases also represent something of an anomaly. The professional judgment standard was initially developed so that courts would not second-guess judgments made by mental health professionals employed by the state. However, in both *Clark* and *Thomas S.*, the state was in the unenviable position of defending itself against decisions made by its own professionals. Thus, mental health professionals working for the state should not be blinded by the lack of treatment alternatives to institutionalization. One question that remains is whether mental health professionals must consider treatment costs when making treatment recommendations. *Clark* held that as long as cost was considered, the treatment recommendation must be followed.

Another question yet to be decided is how much cost has to be considered. For example, if an extremely costly treatment was recommended, would such a treatment decision be considered outside of the realm of ordinary practice and therefore, not entitled to be followed? Just how far professionals can push for services remains unsettled. . . .

Advocacy for Changes in Conditions

Lawsuits filed on behalf of a class of patients for institutional changes have not fared as well as those seeking relief for individual clients. Perhaps because of a fear of protracted involvement with institutions, courts have shown great deference to the professional judgment of those in institutions, even when the conditions and practices may have been suspect. In two cases, courts gave presumptive validity to the standards promulgated by the Joint Commission on Accreditation of Hospitals. However, this presumption can be rebutted by evidence showing abusive practices and neglected conditions.

Accordingly, a second strategy is to advocate for changes in the relevant professional or institutional standards. The standards that regulate the conditions at facilities have long been a source of dispute in institutional litigation cases. The majority of standards detailed by the Joint Commission on Accreditation of Hospitals (and found in judicial consent decrees that order changes in institutional practices) focus on the institutions' physical conditions and operations rather than their therapeutic offerings.

Advocates interested in improving the treatment of children in institutions are advised of two strategies to improve services to institutionalized children. The first is to become aware of the standards that an institution is required to maintain for eligibility as a state and/or federally licensed facility. By monitoring the conditions at facilities, professionals and other advocates can at least insist that children are appropriately cared for and are receiving the care mandated by the standards. . . .

A second, more involved strategy is to work for changes in either the relevant standards or the procedures by which the institutions are monitored to ensure that they are in compliance with the standards. Every state has an agency responsible for monitoring institutions. Such monitoring is a necessary condition of receiving federal monies. Yet the diligence with which states monitor and impose sanctions on facilities that violate standards varies considerably. Advocates interested in ensuring that facilities adhere to standards might contact the state agency responsible for monitoring the facility to check for violations. Although routine checks are made by agencies every year, unscheduled checks may be made if there is probable cause. Finally, if the monitoring process itself is suspect, advocates may contact state protection and advocacy agencies and advise them about possible shortcomings. As required by the Developmental Disabilities Assistance and Bill of Rights Act and the *Protection and Advocacy for Mentally Ill Individuals Act of 1986*, every state now has an independent agency designated to investigate possible rights violations of mentally ill and disabled children.

Litigation aimed at institutional reform and increased services for institutionalized children and adults continues. As this discussion indicates, *Youngberg* and other decisions may have created the opportunity for mental health professionals to obtain better services for individual clients and institute reform at the institutional level. The techniques suggested, however, remain untried. Whether children would realize benefits from such approaches is not clear, and mental health professionals following these recommendations will probably encounter difficulties from institutional administrators. Nonetheless, ethical and humanitarian concerns call for mental health professionals to try these techniques.

> *"The professional judgment standard is akin to a white flag raised by the Court, surrendering those who sought judicial asylum to the tender mercies of professionals whose mandates do not include sensitivity to constitutional rights."*

Judges, Not Mental Health Professionals, Should Make Decisions About the Rights of Patients with Mental Illness

Susan Stefan

At the time this article was written, Susan Stefan was a professor of law at the University of Miami. She is currently an attorney with the Center for Public Representation in Massachusetts. In the following excerpts from a long paper, she argues that in Youngberg v. Romeo *the Supreme Court established the "professional judgment" standard for determining the level of services that a mentally ill person will receive, and that although this may be an appropriate standard when a patient claims to have been denied services, it is not at all appropriate when someone objects to unwanted "services" such as forced treatment. The crucial distinction between an individual's right to receive care from the government and the right to be free of invasive government action has been lost, she says. The Court has ignored the fact that the exercise of professional judgment can invade an individual's constitutional rights. Mental health professionals are*

Susan Stefan, "Leaving Civil Rights to the 'Experts': From Deference to Abdication under the Professional Judgment Standard," *The Yale Law Journal*, vol. 102, 1992, p. 639–717. Copyright © 1992 The Yale Law Journal Company, Inc. Reproduced by permission of the publisher and the author.

not neutral, Stefan explains. On the contrary, they are biased toward treatment, and often institutionalization, at the expense of privacy and liberty. Judges are qualified to make decisions about whether constitutional rights have been violated, and they should not defer to the opinions of professionals.

The United States Supreme Court adopted the professional judgment standard in 1982 in *Youngberg v. Romeo*, a damages action on behalf of a severely mentally retarded man institutionalized at the Pennhurst State School and Hospital in Pennsylvania.... The Court held that individuals confined in state institutions have a right to treatment "which is reasonable in light of [each individual's] identifiable liberty interest" in freedom from unnecessary governmental restraint.... Having made the crucial distinction between negative rights against state intrusion and affirmative rights to government services, however, the Supreme Court proceeded to adopt the same standard, the professional judgment standard, to determine whether there had been a violation of both types of rights. The Court held that a professional's decision is presumptively valid, whether it is challenged as providing inadequate services or as state intrusion on the individual. Professional decisions in the institutional setting are only unconstitutional if "the decision by the professional is such a substantial departure from accepted professional judgment, practice, or standards as to demonstrate that the person responsible actually did not base the decision on such a judgment."

The Professional Judgment Standard

Although the professional judgment standard may be appropriate to measure the level of services that a state is constitutionally bound to provide to individuals in its custody, the standard is inappropriate to justify the imposition of unwanted government "services" that restrict constitutional liberty, such as forcible medication, prolonged restraint, and prohibitions on patients' family visitation. The crucial distinction between an individual's affirmative right to a certain quality of care from the government, and an individual's negative right against invasive state action, is lost under the professional judgment standard, as is the court's crucial role in our constitutional system. By applying the professional judgment standard to negative rights cases, courts cease to protect the "realm of personal liberty which the government may not enter," and instead simply ensure that a professional behaves within the bounds of his profession, regardless of the impact his actions might have on the constitutional rights of the plaintiff. The Court has ignored the reality that the exercise of professional judgment by a state actor can itself invade constitutional rights. The Court has thus abdicated its responsibility to provide a barrier between the individual and unwanted professional intrusion by the state. . . .

Unfortunately, courts have broadened the applicability of the Youngberg doctrine with little regard for what "professional judgment" and the professional judgment standard might actually mean. Instead, courts use the professional judgment standard as a talismanic invocation, rarely examining the predicate assumptions about professionals upon which the standard relies. Courts, particularly the Supreme Court, regard the professional-client relationship as befitting protection from state interference because they envision it as an intimate partnership dedicated to the client's benefit and furtherance of the client's goals. In this popular construction, the archetype of the "professional" is a neutral individual cloaked in expertise, dedicated to a set of objective values, and governed by a higher code of responsibility in his relationship with his clients. This concept of the professional is a myth, yet the courts appear oblivious to the values deeply embedded in professionalism in general and in the medical and mental health professions in particular. Furthermore, neither the idealized values attributed to medical professionals nor their actual perspectives and priorities have much in common with the ideals of autonomy, self-determination, and individualism embodied in the Constitution.

To make matters worse, the courts idealize the wrong group of professionals, basing the professional judgment standard on a powerful mythology about professionals in the private sphere, but almost always applying it in a public sector context. The Court's image of freely chosen professional-client interaction is thus transplanted to institutional settings where the professionals are state actors, the professional-client relationship is permeated with state concerns and conflicts of interest, and the clients are an indigent and captive population. The professional's power in these situations lies not solely or even primarily in his expertise, but in his ability to control every aspect of his clients' lives, including, ultimately, the decision of whether they will be returned to freedom. . . .

When a court classifies a state action as a "professional judgment," the standard prevents the courts from considering the rights at stake in many professional decisions. When it collapses an individual rights claim into an issue of professional judgment, a court abandons the task of weighing the constitutional values that may forbid effectuating the professional's decision. Professionals are neither obligated nor competent to consider these values; this must be the court's role. For example, a Jehovah's Witness's refusal of a blood transfusion may squarely conflict with medical judgment, threatening the patient with death. But such a decision is legally protected for reasons independent of professional medical judgment. Rights do not arise because professionals recommend them, nor are they protected by professional judgment. Constitutional rights transcend professional judgment, and in many respects professional judgment is irrelevant or antithetical to the exercise of these rights. Professional judgment is not concerned with idiosyncratic individual choices about speech, association, religious beliefs, marriage, childbearing, life, and death. Yet the professional judgment standard has transferred the focus of decisionmaking about civil rights to professionals whose expertise, values, and orientation make them unsuitable guardians of those rights. The result is that courts abdicate their fact-finding and decisionmaking responsibilities, creating a significant threat to the preservation of civil rights. And because so many constitutional rights cases can be characterized as confrontations between individuals and government "experts" or "professionals," the professional judgment standard threatens constitutional liberties on many fronts. . . .

The Supreme Court's image of the mental health professional is inaccurate because the assumptions underlying it are far removed from reality. The assumptions are particularly inaccurate and damaging when applied to cases that, like Youngberg, involve indigent patients who must depend for their treatment on professionals employed by the state. Professionals do not in fact act neutrally. Rather, all professionals are shaped by the norms, values, and assumptions of professionalism in general and of their professions in particular. Professional judgment is also inescapably informed by assumptions of class, race, and gender. In addition, professionals who are state actors do not have the same partnership with their clients as do private sector professionals, who are paid by the clients themselves or by private insurance. Duties to the state generate conflicts of interest, and public sector care suffers from severe limitations of resources having few parallels in the private sphere. State institutions often exist primarily for custodial purposes rather than for treatment. Thus, "professional judgment" in state mental health systems takes place under circumstances so far removed from the Court's idealized paradigm of the professional as to make that paradigm unrecognizable and irrelevant.

The Myth of Neutrality

The image that professionals do not impose their own values on their clients and that they have no goals beyond advancing the client's interest is the source of much of their power and a principal reason that professional pronouncements are taken as persuasive. In fact, professionalism is frequently associated with neutrality in case law. In many different ways, however, professionals embody and impose a complex set of values that are far from neutral. In the private sphere a professional's values may be perceived as benign and welcomed by the client; in any event, the client is free to go and select another professional whose values are more consonant with her own. In state institutions, most clients are captive to the values of the professionals who treat them; their only recourse to assert their own values and goals may be a court challenge to the state professional's actions. The courts' failure to grasp the idea that conflict between a professional and a client often involves a clash of value systems leads the courts to apply reflexive presumptions in favor of the professional. Where the clash is evident, as in cases involving religious beliefs and the refusal of blood transfusions, the courts are far less deferential to professionals. The exposure of the value systems underlying professional judgments, then, becomes particularly important.

Members of a given profession often share certain beliefs inculcated as part of their professional training. These beliefs include values common to all professions, such as the notion that the professionals' judgment should be sovereign within their field of expertise. . . . Likewise, all professions share a preference for professional autonomy as against governmental regulation and intervention, whether in the form of legislative requirements or judicial decrees.

Members of a given profession also share values specific to their profession. The legal profession stresses autonomy and individual responsibility, while the medical profession is more paternalistic. In the medical profession, the primary mandate is to cure or restore the health of a patient. When curing or healing a patient conflicts with the patient's own choices, a goal of healing very often supercedes the patient's wishes: patient autonomy is simply not a primary value of the medical profession. Clients in the private sphere, who are relatively more free to consider their doctor's advice in light of their own personal values and to decide the proper course of action for themselves, may expect and appreciate this professional value. The fact that physicians consider treatment and cure to be their first priority should, however, be recognized as a powerful value system that will inevitably skew professional judgment. For example, a physician's doubts about a patient's competence to accept or refuse treatment are typically resolved in the patient's favor if the patient wishes to accept treatment; the patient's competence is challenged only if she refuses treatment. In addition, medical professionals readily sacrifice patient autonomy to protect patients from harm or to reduce risks to their health.

Within the specializations of medicine, each branch also has its own specific set of values, usually (and unsurprisingly) focused on the benefits that the specialists' particular expertise has to offer. For example, physicians at institutions tend to resolve doubts in favor of institutional care. . . .

The Myth That Professional Judgment Transcends Public/Private Distinctions

The Supreme Court acknowledged in Youngberg that state hospitals are often "overcrowded and understaffed" and explicitly stated that one purpose of the professional judgment standard was to "enable institutions of this type . . . to continue to function." Yet professional judgment, as envisioned by the Supreme Court, is distorted beyond recognition by the limited resources, coercive environment, and unavoidable conflicts of interest inherent in the public sector. Professionals employed by the state are state actors. Those who work in state institutions have conflicting obligations: to the state, whose budgetary demands restrict state employees' behavior; to the institution, which might be more concerned about safety and security than treatment; and to the patients, who did not seek their care and who, for the most part, have no desire to be patients in the first place. The Supreme Court has generally not acknowledged this conflict and, when parties have raised the issue, has responded with the assumption that professionalism will serve as a prophylactic against any pressure created by state employment: state actors who are professionals are assumed to act with "professional" intent or motives rather than "state" intent or motives.

The health care professional's values regarding the primacy of treatment become particularly troubling when the professional is a state actor and the state has custody over the patient, for then the professional's already considerable power over the patient is joined with the power of the state. At that point, the professional's orientation to treatment must be recognized as a value system in itself, rather than as a neutral, value-free description of what is required. . . .

Furthermore, the exercise of professional judgment under the conditions prevailing in state institutions may often be impossible, as even the Court itself has acknowledged. When the Supreme Court agreed to hear Youngberg, it already knew about Pennhurst's abysmal record, having recently decided a case involving that very institution. Justice Rehnquist wrote, "[The District Court's] findings of fact are undisputed: Conditions at Pennhurst are not only dangerous, with the residents often physically abused or drugged by staff members, but also inadequate for the 'habilitation' of the retarded." . . .

The professional judgment framework reformulates all constitutional questions into a dichotomy between professional judgment and its absence, and thus renders irrelevant those values that transcend the issue of professionalism. An action may be well within the norms of professional judgment and at the same time violate constitutional rights to freedom from physical violence, bodily intrusion, punishment, interference with the parent-child relationship, or limitations of speech or religion. A finding that professional judgment was followed thus has little if any relevance to the protection of civil rights; courts need to look beyond the professional recommendation to the effect of state action on an individual's rights.

Right to Refuse Treatment

The law is clear that a competent individual outside government custody cannot be treated against her will; the Supreme Court probably raised this rule to the level of a constitutional right in *Cruzan v. Director, Missouri Department of Health*. Most state courts have applied this holding equally to institutionalized persons, requiring a judicial finding of incompetency before an individual can be treated against her will; and many institutionalized individuals in fact remain competent to make treatment decisions. Federal constitutional law, however, follows the professional judgment standard, which requires no showing as to the patient's competence, condition with or without medication, or need for treatment. Nor is it necessary to show that the proposed treatment will be effective, that medication is the least restrictive alternative, or even that any treatment alternatives have been considered or attempted in treating the patient. Certainly, no hearing is required. Rather, the constitutional right of institutionalized patients to refuse antipsychotic medications can be overridden under current law by a showing that the physician has not substantially departed from professional judgment in ordering forced medication.

The professional may well be correct in regarding the treatment as effective and thus may be exercising the best professional judgment in forcibly medicating the patient. But this judicial approach fails to consider—indeed, it does not even articulate—the competing values at stake. These values have been readily recognized in other decisions involving refusals of medical treatment recommended by a treating professional, such as blood transfusions violating the religious beliefs of the patient.

Individuals refusing treatment do not seek services or challenge the quality of treatment. Their claim is to be protected from state intrusions in the name of treatment. The professional judgment standard is meaningless in this context. It may be appropriate to use the professional judgment standard to decide whether an institutionalized or imprisoned patient is constitutionally entitled to a particular treatment program or to a certain medication or drug, such as AZT. But to apply the identical standard to determine the constitutionality of forcing AZT or some other medication on an unwilling patient misses the enormous distinction between the two scenarios. The professional judgment standard does not distinguish between treatment requested and treatment refused. Furthermore, because the focus is on the professional's judgment rather than on the legal claim, no distinction is made between "treatments" such as restraints that implicate traditional liberty interests in freedom of movement and more benign treatments such as basket weaving and pottery classes.

Behavior Modification: Punishment, Liberty, and Professional Judgment

Behavior modification is a central goal of many mental disability professionals, especially those dealing with mental retardation. It is also used with juveniles, particularly in the area of juvenile justice. Cases involving behavior modification programs represent a particularly good example of the importance of distinguishing between negative and affirmative constitutional claims. In some of these cases, plaintiffs assert a constitutional right to behavior modification programs as treatment. In others, plaintiffs seek judicial protection from behavior modification programs that they claim infringe their liberty; these negative rights cases call for a different analysis than the affirmative rights cases. Yet the professional judgment standard as presently applied does not admit this distinction.

Where plaintiffs have asserted an affirmative right to behavior modification programs, courts have appropriately looked to the professional judgment standard and found such programs constitutionally required. The professional judgment standard has not yet been applied to behavior modification programs in negative rights cases because plaintiffs are not bringing federal constitutional challenges to behavior modification programs in state institutions. In this author's experience, mental health lawyers do not litigate such claims because they assume they would fail under the professional judgment standard. This is probably correct, because behavior modification is a widely accepted professional practice. Yet looking simply to professional judgment would miss the crux of such negative rights claims.

In constitutional challenges to behavior modification programs, plaintiffs do not challenge the programs' professional adequacy; rather, they demand freedom from punishment, bodily restraint, or even assert the right to adequate food, clothing and shelter. In the name of behavior modification, clients have been denied access to food, religious services, and visitation with their families. . . .

Programs of aversive therapy and behavior modification are certainly within the realm of professional judgment. Professionals rely on the effectiveness of these programs to extinguish target behaviors. However, by evaluating a program solely on the basis of whether its use departs from professional judgment, a court ignores the individual rights at stake. . . .

When a mental patient is intentionally subjected to harsh conditions in order to deter him from maintaining a course of conduct, the fact that it is done in the name of psychiatric treatment does not keep it from being intentional punishment. The importance of the court's role in protecting individuals from state intrusion—and the inability of the professional judgment standard to accomplish this end—can be seen by considering the consequences if the professional judgment standard were to be adopted in cases alleging illegal search and seizure, psychologically coerced confessions, or police entrapment. Many such actions could be considered professionally acceptable police practices, but citizens' rights against police intrusion would be greatly diminished if professional acceptability from the standpoint of the police were all that the Constitution required. Courts are often blind to this argument in cases involving behavior modification and other treatment practices of professionals primarily because of the images that judges associate with professionalism. Courts are unaccustomed to connecting the word "treatment" with an unwilling patient compelled to submit to professional ministrations. To the courts, "treatment" does not connote an adversarial relationship. But in negative rights cases, the professional and patient are adversaries, and the court must rely upon constitutional doctrines and values, rather than on professional values, to resolve the dispute. . . .

Constitutional Rights

The problem with defining a professional as "a person competent, whether by education, training or experience, to make the particular decision at issue" is that this definition transforms the court's understanding of both "the decision at issue" and who should properly be making it. Thus courts recast questions of law as questions of fact, which, in turn, will necessarily be regarded as the province of "professionals" to whom the court should defer. The decision properly at issue in *Youngberg v. Romeo*, for example, was not the clinical one of whether Romeo should have been restrained, but the constitutional one of whether the imposed physical restraints, regardless of clinical efficacy or indication, violated his constitutional rights. The clinical decision is one that professionals, unconstrained by budgetary problems and conflicts of interest, would presumably be qualified to make. The legal decision is one that judges are not only qualified but also required to make in order to preserve liberties guaranteed by the Constitution. While judges may need to inquire into the clinical or professional rationale underlying the decision to restrain in order to make a decision regarding constitutionality, that rationale should not form the substance of the constitutional standard.

An evaluation of the restraints' propriety in terms of clinical standards may be relevant to the relationship between government purposes and the means used to achieve those purposes. Clinical standards cannot and should not, however, be transmuted into constitutional values, and satisfying them cannot be equated with fulfilling constitutional norms. As Justice Blackmun noted in a case challenging prison regulations, "I am concerned about the Court's apparent willingness to substitute the rhetoric of judicial deference for meaningful scrutiny of constitutional claims. . . . The fact that particular measures advance prison security . . . does not make them ipso facto constitutional." Freedom from bodily restraint, like freedom from governmental intervention in general, may not be in the best interests of the individual, especially in the judgment of others. The exercise of free speech may also be counter-therapeutic. Indeed, many great Supreme Court decisions have transcended some professional's judgment in order to vindicate an individual's constitutional rights. . . .

The claim of an individual seeking relief from government intrusion on her rights is not answered by the assurance that the state action arose from a professional judgment. For institutionalized people and other unwilling clients, this assurance amounts to no more than a constitutional right to have professional judgment exercised on their behalf in exchange for

143

all their other rights. Rights to privacy, free speech, freedom from unreasonable search and seizure, and Due Process are extinguished at the will of professionals exercising their judgments in the name of appropriate treatment.

In cases in which the constitutional claim is that the plaintiff was entitled to professional judgment and did not receive it, such as claims of ineffective assistance of counsel, claims for treatment, or claims for services in foster care, the professional judgment standard is an appropriate benchmark. But when the plaintiff seeks refuge in the courts to protect her autonomy from intrusions by state professionals—to protect the manifold idiosyncrasies and acts of courage that the Bill of Rights and the Fourteenth Amendment shield from the professional ministrations of the majoritarian state—then the professional judgment standard is akin to a white flag raised by the Court, surrendering those who sought judicial asylum to the tender mercies of professionals whose mandates do not include sensitivity to constitutional rights.

CHAPTER 4

The Right to Live
and Receive Treatment
in the Community

Case Overview

Olmstead v. L.C. and E.W. (1999)

Lois Curtis and Elaine Wilson were mentally retarded women, both of whom also had mild forms of mental illness. In 1993 Curtis, who had been in mental hospitals previously, was voluntarily admitted to the Georgia Regional Hospital (GRH), where she was confined for treatment in a psychiatric unit. A year later her doctors agreed that she had improved enough to be released from the hospital to one of the community-based programs the state of Georgia supported. In spite of this she remained institutionalized for another three years. In 1995 Wilson was also voluntarily admitted to GRH and confined. GRH tried to send her to a homeless shelter but gave up that plan when her attorney complained. The next year her psychiatrist decided that she, too, could be treated appropriately in a community-based setting, but Wilson was not released from GRH.

Because of the way state financing of mental health care is arranged, mentally ill or retarded patients often remain confined in mental institutions after their doctors have approved their discharge. If certain funds have been allocated to a mental hospital, less funding may be available for community-based treatment programs. It may be simpler to keep the mentally disabled in institutions than to give them the help they need outside. Many people believe that this practice constitutes a serious violation of civil rights.

In May 1995, while she was still institutionalized at GRH, Curtis contacted the Atlanta Legal Aid Society. The group helped her file a lawsuit against the state of Georgia challenging her continued confinement in a segregated environment and requesting she receive treatment with the ultimate goal of integrating her into the mainstream of society. Wilson joined the suit. (Both women were identified only by initials in the lawsuit's title, but their names have since been made public.) The suit claimed that keeping them in a hospital violated the Americans with Disabilities Act (ADA), a law designed to prevent disabled people from being treated differently from those without disabilities.

The district court ruled in favor of the two women. It rejected the state of Georgia's argument that inadequate funding, not discrimination against them because of their disabilities, accounted for their retention at GRH. The court concluded that "unnecessary institutional segregation of the disabled constitutes discrimination per se, which cannot be justified by a lack of funding." It also affirmed that existing state programs offered community-based treatment of the kind for which Curtis and Wilson qualified and that the state could "provide services to plaintiffs in the community at considerably less cost than is required to maintain them in an institution."

The court of appeals agreed with the judgment of the district court, holding that when "a disabled individual's treating professionals find that a community-based placement is appropriate for that individual, the ADA imposes a duty to provide treatment in a community setting—the most integrated setting appropriate to that patient's needs." The court held, however, that "fundamental alterations" of a state's services to mental patients were not required if providing community-based treatment would be unreasonably costly.

The Supreme Court agreed to review the case because of its importance to the states and to the affected individuals. By that time both women had been released as ordered by the lower court and were receiving community services, but the state of Georgia had not changed its general policy with regard to its patients. Furthermore, the outcome of the suit would affect not only people with mental disabilities, but also those with physical disabilities. For that reason disability activists of many kinds united to make their need for freedom from institutionalization known to the Supreme Court.

The justices of the Supreme Court were divided in their opinion on the Case, but majority agreed that segregating disabled people constitutes discrimination. Only four judges held that lack of funding could, in some cases, excuse a state from providing community-based services, and the opinion left open the question of what circumstances would justify forcing states to provide these services.

> *"Institutional placement of persons who can handle and benefit from community settings perpetuates unwarranted assumptions that persons so isolated are incapable or unworthy of participating in community life."*

The Court's Decision: Patients Eligible for Community-Based Treatment Cannot Be Kept in Institutions Against Their Will

Ruth Bader Ginsburg

Ruth Bader Ginsburg has been a justice of the Supreme Court since 1993 and is one of its most liberal members. The following viewpoint is the majority opinion of the Court in Olmstead v. L.C. and E.W., *in which it ruled that keeping disabled individuals in institutions when they are capable of living outside is a violation of the Americans with Disabilities Act (ADA). Isolation of such individuals constitutes discrimination, she says, even though they are not denied community services "by reason of" their disabilities. The Court believed that when Congress wrote the ADA it intended segregation of the disabled to be viewed as a form of discrimination. The opinion also noted, however, that it would not be reasonable to require states to provide community-abused care for a few individuals when the cost is high compared to the total amount spent on mental health. Thus, Ginsburg states, the ADA requires states to provide*

Ruth Bader Ginsburg, majority opinion, *Tommy Olmstead, Commissioner, Georgia Department of Human Resources et al., v. L.C., by Jonathan Zimring, guardian ad litem, et al.*, U. S. Supreme Court, June 22, 1999.

community-based treatment where it is appropriate, but the resources of the state and the needs of other patients must be considered.

This case concerns the proper construction of the anti-discrimination provision contained in the public services portion (Title II) of the Americans with Disabilities Act of 1990. Specifically, we confront the question whether the proscription of discrimination may require placement of persons with mental disabilities in community settings rather than in institutions. The answer, we hold, is a qualified yes. Such action is in order when the State's treatment professionals have determined that community placement is appropriate, the transfer from institutional care to a less restrictive setting is not opposed by the affected individual, and the placement can be reasonably accommodated, taking into account the resources available to the State and the needs of others with mental disabilities. . . .

This case, as it comes to us, presents no constitutional question. The complaints filed by plaintiffs-respondents L. C. and E. W. did include such an issue; L. C. and E. W. alleged that defendants-petitioners, Georgia health care officials, failed to afford them minimally adequate care and freedom from undue restraint, in violation of their rights under the Due Process Clause of the Fourteenth Amendment. But neither the District Court nor the Court of Appeals reached those Fourteenth Amendment claims. Instead, the courts below resolved the case solely on statutory grounds. Our review is similarly confined. Mindful that it is a statute we are construing, we set out first the legislative and regulatory prescriptions on which the case turns.

In the opening provisions of the ADA, Congress stated findings applicable to the statute in all its parts. Most relevant to this case, Congress determined that

(2) historically, society has tended to isolate and segregate individuals with disabilities, and, despite some improvements, such forms of discrimination against individuals with disabilities continue to be a serious and pervasive social problem;

(3) discrimination against individuals with disabilities persists in such critical areas as . . . institutionalization . . . ;

(5) individuals with disabilities continually encounter various forms of discrimination, including outright intentional exclusion, . . . failure to make modifications to existing facilities and practices, . . . [and] segregation. . . .

Congress then set forth prohibitions against discrimination in employment, public services furnished by governmental entities, and public accommodations provided by private entities. The statute as a whole is intended "to provide a clear and comprehensive national mandate for the elimination of discrimination against individuals with disabilities."

ADA Public Services Regulations

This case concerns Title II, the public services portion of the ADA. The provision of Title II centrally at issue reads:

"Subject to the provisions of this subchapter, no qualified individual with a disability shall, by reason of such disability, be excluded from participation in or be denied the benefits of the services, programs, or activities of a public entity, or be subjected to discrimination by any such entity." . . .

As Congress instructed, the Attorney General issued Title II regulations, including one modeled on the regulation just quoted; called the "integration regulation," it reads: "A public entity shall administer services, programs, and activities in the most integrated setting appropriate to the needs of qualified individuals with disabilities."

The preamble to the Attorney General's Title II regulations defines "the most integrated setting appropriate to the needs of qualified individuals with disabilities" to mean "a setting that enables individuals with disabilities to interact with non-disabled persons to the fullest extent possible." Another regulation requires public entities to "make reasonable modifications" to avoid "discrimination on the basis of disability," unless those modifications would entail a "fundamenta[l] alter[ation]"; called here the "reasonable-modifications regulation," it provides:

> A public entity shall make reasonable modifications in policies, practices, or procedures when the modifications are necessary to avoid discrimination on the basis of disability, unless the public entity can demonstrate that making the modifications would fundamentally alter the nature of the service, program, or activity.

We recite these regulations with the caveat that we do not here determine their validity. While the parties differ on the proper construction and enforcement of the regulations, we do not understand petitioners to challenge the regulatory formulations themselves as outside the congressional authorization. . . .

Discrimination Based on Disability

We affirm the Court of Appeals' decision in substantial part. Unjustified isolation, we hold, is properly regarded as discrimination based on disability. But we recognize, as well, the States' need to maintain a range of facilities for the care and treatment of persons with diverse mental disabilities, and the States' obligation to administer services with an even hand. Accordingly, we further hold that the Court of Appeals' remand instruction was unduly restrictive. In evaluating a State's fundamental-alteration defense, the District Court must consider, in view of the resources available to the State, not only the cost of providing community-based care to the litigants, but also the range of services the State provides others with mental disabilities, and the State's obligation to mete out those services equitably.

We examine first whether, as the Eleventh Circuit held, undue institutionalization qualifies as discrimination "by reason of . . . disability." The Department of Justice has consistently advocated that it does. Because the Department is the agency directed by Congress to issue, regulations implementing Title II, its views warrant respect. . . .

The State argues that L. C. and E. W. encountered no discrimination "by reason of" their disabilities because they were not denied community placement on account of those disabilities. Nor were they subjected to "discrimination," the State contends, because "'discrimination' necessarily requires uneven treatment of similarly situated individuals," and L. C. and E. W. had identified no comparison class, i.e., no similarly situated individuals given preferential treatment. We are satisfied that Congress had a more comprehensive view of the concept of discrimination advanced in the ADA.

The ADA stepped up earlier measures to secure opportunities for people with developmental disabilities to enjoy the benefits of community living. The Developmentally Disabled Assistance and Bill of Rights Act (DDABRA), a 1975 measure, stated in aspirational terms that "[t]he treatment, services, and habilitation for a person with developmental disabilities . . . should be provided in the setting that is least restrictive of the person's personal liberty." In a related legislative endeavor, the Rehabilitation Act of 1973, Congress used mandatory language to proscribe discrimination against persons with disabilities. Ultimately, in the ADA, enacted in 1990, Congress not only required all public entities to refrain from discrimination, additionally, in findings applicable to the entire statute, Congress explicitly identified unjustified "segregation" of persons with disabilities as a "for[m] of discrimination."

Recognition that unjustified institutional isolation of persons with disabilities is a form of discrimination reflects two evident judgments. First, institutional placement of persons who can handle and benefit from community settings perpetuates unwarranted assumptions that persons so isolated are incapable or unworthy of participating in community life. Second, confinement in an institution severely diminishes the everyday life activities of individuals, including family relations, social contacts, work options, economic independence, educational advancement, and cultural enrichment. Dissimilar treatment correspondingly exists in this key respect: In order to receive needed medical services, persons with mental disabilities must, because of those disabilities, relinquish participation in community life they could enjoy given reasonable accommodations, while persons without mental disabilities can receive the medical services they need without similar sacrifice.

The State urges that, whatever Congress may have stated as its findings in the ADA, the Medicaid statute "reflected a congressional policy preference for treatment in the institution over treatment in the community." The State correctly used the past tense. Since 1981, Medicaid has provided funding for state-run home and community-based care through a waiver program. Indeed, the United States points out that the Department of Health and Human Services (HHS) "has a policy of encouraging States to take advantage of the waiver program, and often approves more waiver slots than a State ultimately uses."

We emphasize that nothing in the ADA or its implementing regulations condones termination of institutional settings for persons unable to handle or benefit from community settings. Title II provides only that "qualified individual[s] with a disability" may not "be subjected to discrimination." "Qualified individuals," the ADA further explains, are persons with disabilities who, "with or without reasonable modifications to rules, policies, or practices, . . . mee[t] the essential eligibility requirements for the receipt of services or the participation in programs or activities provided by a public entity."

Consistent with these provisions, the State generally may rely on the reasonable assessments of its own professionals in determining whether an individual "meets the essential eligibility requirements" for habilitation in a community-based program. Absent such qualification, it would be inappropriate to remove a patient from the more restrictive setting. Nor is there any federal requirement that community-based treatment be imposed on patients who do not desire it. In this case, however, there is no genuine dispute concerning the status of L. C. and E. W. as individuals "qualified" for noninstitutional care: The State's own professionals determined that community-based treatment would be appropriate for L. C. and E. W., and neither woman opposed such treatment.

Cost Considerations

The State's responsibility, once it provides community-based treatment to qualified persons with disabilities, is not boundless. The reasonable modifications regulation speaks of "reasonable modifications" to avoid discrimination, and allows States to resist modifications that entail a "fundamenta[l] alter[ation]" of the States' services and programs. The Court of Appeals construed this regulation to permit a cost-based defense "only in the most limited of circumstances," and remanded to the District Court to consider, among other things, "whether the additional expenditures necessary to treat L. C. and E. W. in community-based care would be unreasonable given the demands of the State's mental health budget."

The Court of Appeals' construction of the reasonable-modifications regulation is unacceptable for it would leave the State virtually defenseless once it is shown that the plaintiff is qualified for the service or program she seeks. If the expense entailed in placing one or two people in a community-based treatment program is properly measured for reasonableness against the State's entire mental health budget, it is unlikely that a State, relying on the fundamental-alteration defense, could ever prevail. Sensibly construed, the fundamental-alteration component of the reasonable-modifications regulation would allow the State to show that, in the allocation of available resources, immediate relief for the plaintiffs would be inequitable, given the responsibility the State has undertaken for the care and treatment of a large and diverse population of persons with mental disabilities. When it granted summary judgment for plaintiffs in this case, the District Court compared the cost of caring for the plaintiffs in a community-based setting with the cost of caring for them in an institution. That simple comparison showed that community placements cost less than institutional confinements. As the United States recognizes, however, a comparison so simple overlooks costs the State cannot avoid; most notably, a "State . . . may experience increased overall expenses by funding community placements without being able to take advantage of the savings associated with the closure of institutions." *Brief for United States as Amicus Curiae.*

As already observed, the ADA is not reasonably read to impel States to phase out institutions, placing patients in need of close care at risk. Nor is it the ADA's mission to drive States to move institutionalized patients into an inappropriate setting, such as a homeless shelter, a placement the State proposed, then retracted, for E. W. Some individuals, like L. C. and E. W. in prior years, may need institutional care from time to time "to stabilize acute psychiatric symptoms." (affidavit of Dr. Richard L. Elliott). For other individuals, no placement outside the institution may ever be appropriate.

To maintain a range of facilities and to administer services with an even hand, the State must have more leeway than the courts below understood the fundamental-alteration defense to allow. If, for example, the State were to demonstrate that it had a comprehensive, effectively working plan for placing qualified persons with mental disabilities in less restrictive settings, and a waiting list that moved at a reasonable pace not controlled by the State's endeavors to keep its institutions fully populated, the reasonable-modifications standard would be met. In such circumstances, a court would have no warrant effectively to order displacement of persons at the top of the community-based treatment waiting list by individuals lower down who commenced civil actions.

For the reasons stated, we conclude that, under Title II of the ADA, States are required to provide community-based treatment for persons with mental disabilities when the State's treatment professionals determine that such placement is appropriate, the affected persons do not oppose such treatment, and the placement can be reasonably accommodated, taking into account the resources available to the State and the needs of others with mental disabilities.

> "We cannot expand the meaning of the term 'discrimination' in order to invalidate policies we may find unfortunate."

Dissenting Opinion: Treating Different Patients Differently Is Not Disability-Based Discrimination

Clarence Thomas

Clarence Thomas, the second African American to serve on the Supreme Court, has been a justice since 1991. He is among the Court's most conservative members. The following viewpoint is his dissenting opinion in Olmstead v. L.C., *in which the Court decided that disabled persons should not be kept in institutions against their will if their doctors believed their needs could be met by community-based services. Thomas argues that to call this discrimination is to give the term a meaning different from its ordinary one. Discrimination, he says, has always meant treating a person differently from members of a different group on the basis of the group to which that person belongs. It has not included different treatment of different individuals within the same group. Furthermore, he argues, disabled persons able to live outside are not kept in institutions "by reason of" their disabilities, but merely because community-based services are not available for them.*

Clarence Thomas, dissenting opinion, *Tommy Olmstead, Commissioner, Georgia Department of Human Resources et al., v. L.C., by Jonathan Zimring, guardian ad litem, et al.,* U. S. Supreme Court, June 22, 1999.

Title II of the Americans with Disabilities Act of 1990 (ADA), provides: "Subject to the provisions of this subchapter, no qualified individual with a disability shall, by reason of such disability, be excluded from participation in or be denied the benefits of the services, programs, or activities of a public entity, or be subjected to discrimination by any such entity."

The majority concludes that petitioners "discriminated" against respondents as a matter of law by continuing to treat them in an institutional setting after they became eligible for community placement. I disagree. Temporary exclusion from community placement does not amount to "discrimination" in the traditional sense of the word, nor have respondents shown that petitioners "discriminated" against them "by reason of" their disabilities.

Until today, this Court has never endorsed an interpretation of the term "discrimination" that encompassed disparate treatment among members of the same protected class. Discrimination, as typically understood, requires a showing that a claimant received differential treatment vis-a-vis members of a different group on the basis of a statutorily described characteristic. This interpretation comports with dictionary definitions of the term discrimination, which means to "distinguish," to "differentiate," or to make a "distinction in favor of or against, a person or thing based on the group, class, or category to which that person or thing belongs rather than on individual merit."

Our decisions construing various statutory prohibitions against "discrimination" have not wavered from this path. . . .

Under Title VII, a finding of discrimination requires a comparison of otherwise similarly situated persons who are in different groups by reason of certain characteristics provided by statute.

For this reason, we have described as "nonsensical" the comparison of the racial composition of different classes of

159

job categories in determining whether there existed disparate impact discrimination with respect to a particular job category. Courts interpreting Title VII have held that a plaintiff cannot prove "discrimination" by demonstrating that one member of a particular protected group has been favored over another member of that same group. See, e.g., *Bush v. Commonwealth Edison Co.*, (explaining that under Title VII, a fired black employee "had to show that although he was not a good employee, equally bad employees were treated more leniently by [his employer] if they happened not to be black"). Our cases interpreting Section 504 of the Rehabilitation Act of 1973, as amended, which prohibits "discrimination" against certain individuals with disabilities, have applied this commonly understood meaning of discrimination. Section 504 provides: "No otherwise qualified handicapped individual shall, solely by reason of his handicap, be excluded from the participation in, be denied the benefits of, or be subjected to discrimination under any program or activity receiving Federal financial assistance."

The Definition of Discrimination

In keeping with the traditional paradigm, we have always limited the application of the term "discrimination" in the Rehabilitation Act to a person who is a member of a protected group and faces discrimination "by reason of his handicap." Indeed, we previously rejected the argument that Section 504 requires the type of "affirmative efforts to overcome the disabilities caused by handicaps," *Southeastern Community College v. Davis*, that the majority appears to endorse today. Instead, we found that Section 504 required merely "the evenhanded treatment of handicapped persons" relative to those persons who do not have disabilities. Our conclusion was informed by the fact that some provisions of the Rehabilitation Act envision "affirmative action" on behalf of those individuals with disabilities, but Section 504 itself "does not refer at all" to such action. Therefore, "[a] comparison of these provisions demonstrates that Congress understood accommodation of the needs of handicapped individuals may require affirmative action and knew how to provide for it in those instances where it wished to do so."

Similarly, in *Alexander v. Choate*, we found no discrimination under Section 504 with respect to a limit on inpatient hospital care that was "neutral on its face" and did not "distinguish between those whose coverage will be reduced and those whose coverage will not on the basis of any test, judgment, or trait that the handicapped as a class are less capable of meeting or less likely of having." We said that Section 504 does "not guarantee the handicapped equal results from the provision of state Medicaid, even assuming some measure of equality of health could be constructed."

Likewise, in *Traynor v. Turnage*, we reiterated that the purpose of Section 504 is to guarantee that individuals with disabilities receive "evenhanded treatment" relative to those persons without disabilities. In *Traynor*, the Court upheld a Veterans' Administration regulation that excluded "primary alcoholics" from a benefit that was extended to persons disabled by alcoholism related to a mental disorder. In so doing, the Court noted that, "[t]his litigation does not involve a program or activity that is alleged to treat handicapped persons less favorably than nonhandicapped persons." Given the theory of the case, the Court explicitly held: "There is nothing in the Rehabilitation Act that requires that any benefit extended to one category of handicapped persons also be extended to all other categories of handicapped persons."

This same understanding of discrimination also informs this Court's constitutional interpretation of the term.

The Intent of Congress

Despite this traditional understanding, the majority derives a more "capacious" definition of "discrimination," as that term is used in Title II of the ADA, one that includes "institutional isolation of persons with disabilities." It chiefly relies on certain congressional findings contained within the ADA. To be sure, those findings appear to equate institutional isolation with segregation, and thereby discrimination. The congressional findings, however, are written in general, hortatory terms and provide little guidance to the interpretation of the specific language of [the law]. In my view, the vague congressional findings upon which the majority relies simply do not suffice to show that Congress sought to overturn a well-established understanding of a statutory term (here, "discrimination").

Moreover, the majority fails to explain why terms in the findings should be given a medical content, pertaining to the place where a mentally retarded person is treated. When read in context, the findings instead suggest that terms such as "segregation" were used in a more general sense, pertaining to matters such as access to employment, facilities, and transportation. Absent a clear directive to the contrary, we must read "discrimination" in light of the common understanding of the term. We cannot expand the meaning of the term "discrimination" in order to invalidate policies we may find unfortunate.

Elsewhere in the ADA, Congress chose to alter the traditional definition of discrimination. Title I of the ADA, defines discrimination to include "limiting, segregating, or classifying a job applicant or employee in a way that adversely affects the opportunities or status of such applicant or employee." Notably, however, Congress did not provide that this definition of discrimination, unlike other aspects of the ADA, applies to Title II. Ordinary canons of construction require that we respect the limited applicability of this definition of "discrimination" and not import it into other parts of the law where Congress did not see fit. The majority's definition of discrimination although not specifically delineated substantially imports the definition of Title I into Title II by necessarily assuming that it is sufficient to focus exclusively on members of one particular group. Under this view, discrimination occurs when some members of a protected group are treated differently from other members of that same group. As the preceding discussion emphasizes, absent a special definition supplied by Congress, this conclusion is a remarkable and novel proposition that finds no support in our decisions in analogous areas. For example, the majority's conclusion that petitioners "discriminated" against respondents is the equivalent to finding discrimination under Title VII where a black employee with deficient management skills is denied in-house training by his employer (allegedly because of lack of funding) because other similarly situated black employees are given the in-house training. Such a claim would fly in the face of our prior case law, which requires more than the assertion that a person belongs to a protected group and did not receive some benefit.

At bottom, the type of claim approved of by the majority does not concern a prohibition against certain conduct (the traditional understanding of discrimination), but rather imposition of a standard of care. As such, the majority can offer no principle limiting this new species of "discrimination" claim apart from an affirmative defense because it looks merely to an individual in isolation, without comparing him to otherwise similarly situated persons, and determines that discrimination occurs merely because that individual does not receive the treatment he wishes to receive. By adopting such a broad view of discrimination, the majority drains the term of any meaning other than as a proxy for decisions disapproved of by this Court.

Interference with State Governments

Further, I fear that the majority's approach imposes significant federalism costs, directing States how to make decisions about their delivery of public services. We previously have recognized that constitutional principles of federalism erect limits on the Federal Government's ability to direct state officers or to interfere with the functions of state governments. We have suggested that these principles specifically apply to whether States are required to provide a certain level of benefits to individuals with disabilities. As noted in *Alexander*, in rejecting a similar theory under Section 504 of the Rehabilitation Act: "[N]othing suggests that Congress desired to make major inroads on the States' longstanding discretion to choose the proper mix of amount, scope, and duration limitations on services." The majority's affirmative defense will likely come as cold comfort to the States that will now be forced to defend themselves in federal court every time resources prevent the immediate placement of a qualified individual. In keeping with our traditional deference in this area, the appropriate course would be to respect the States' historical role as the dominant authority responsible for providing services to individuals with disabilities.

The majority may remark that it actually does properly compare members of different groups. Indeed, the majority mentions in passing the "[d]issimilar treatment" of persons with and without disabilities. It does so in the context of supporting its conclusion that institutional isolation is a form of discrimination. It cites two cases as standing for the unremarkable proposition that discrimination leads to deleterious stereotyping, *Los Angeles Dept of Water and Power v. Manhart*, and an amicus brief which indicates that confinement diminishes certain everyday life activities. The majority then observes that persons without disabilities "can receive the services they need without" institutionalization and thereby avoid these twin deleterious effects. I do not quarrel with the two general propositions, but I fail to see how they assist in resolving the issue before the Court. Further, the majority neither specifies what services persons with disabilities might need, nor contends that persons without disabilities need the same services as those with disabilities, leading to the inference that the dissimilar treatment the majority observes results merely from the fact that different classes of persons receive different services not from "discrimination" as traditionally defined.

Finally, it is also clear petitioners did not "discriminate" against respondents "by reason of [their] disabili[ties]," as [the law] requires. We have previously interpreted the phrase "by reason of" as requiring proximate causation. Such an interpretation is in keeping with the vernacular understanding of the phrase. This statute should be read as requiring proximate causation as well. Respondents do not contend that their disabilities constituted the proximate cause for their exclusion. Nor could they; community placement simply is not available to those without disabilities. Continued institutional treatment of persons who, though now deemed treatable in a community placement, must wait their turn for placement, does not establish that the denial of community placement occurred "by reason of" their disability. Rather, it establishes no more than the fact that petitioners have limited resources.

| *"Like all of us, L.C. and E.W. wish to live in freedom, not be incarcerated for the crime of having a disability."*

Disability-Rights Activists Demanded the Right Not to Be Institutionalized

Nadina LaSpina

Nadina LaSpina, who is physically disabled, is a disability-rights activist. She wrote the following viewpoint for a disability rights magazine when Olmstead v. L.C. and E.W. *was pending before the Supreme Court, pointing out that the outcome of the case would affect not only mentally disabled people but also those with physical disabilities. Many states were opposing the right of capable disabled people not to be institutionalized, she says, and in her opinion for them to win would seriously weaken the Americans with Disabilities Act. She describes the ways in which organizations advocating disability rights were mobilizing their members to make the Supreme Court justices aware of the importance of giving the disabled the freedom to live where they choose. She argues that it was a good thing that people with different types of disabilities were getting together in this effort and coming to understand each others' problems.*

We are facing right now the worst threat yet to our civil rights: the *Olmstead* case. The outcome of *Olmstead v. L.C. and E.W.* will determine if we have the right to choose whether we live in our homes or in institutions—or if the

Nadina LaSpina, "Don't Tread on the ADA, Integration NOT Segregation!" *DIA Activist*, January 1999. Reproduced by permission.

states will make that choice for us. And it will determine if the ADA [Americans with Disabilities Act] protects our right to integration—or if the states are free to ignore the ADA's mandate.

Who is Olmstead? Who are L.C. and E.W.? Olmstead is "Thomas Olmstead," Commissioner of Human Resources for the State of Georgia. L.C. and E.W. are two women from Georgia (Lois Curtis and Elaine Wilson). Both have mild retardation, and, in addition, carry the labels of psychiatric diagnoses. Like all of us, L.C. and E.W. wish to live in freedom, not be incarcerated for the crime of having a disability. So when they found themselves locked up in a state hospital, they sued the state, claiming that, under ADA /Title II, they had "the right to receive services in the most integrated setting"—in their homes, in the community. In April 1998, they won their case in the Northern Georgia U.S. District Court, and when the State appealed, they won again in the 11th Circuit Court. Then the state of Georgia appealed its case to the U.S. Supreme Court.

The Supreme Court has until now refused to hear appeals of cases based on the ADA integration mandate, indicating agreement with that interpretation of the law. The first such case was *Helen L. v. DiDario* in Pennsylvania. Helen L., a woman with physical disabilities, charged that placement in a nursing home violated her rights under the ADA, since the personal assistance services she needed could and should be provided in her home, in the community. Argued and won by attorney Steve Gold in 1995, the *Helen L.* decision was a landmark victory for the disability community. Since *Helen L.*, the argument that, under the ADA, we have "the right to receive services in the most integrated setting" has been used over and over to "free our people" from nursing homes and other institutions.

But the Supreme Court has agreed to hear *Olmstead v. L.C. and E.W.* Why? Because the state of Georgia has been getting the support of the whole nation. State legislatures, governors, mayors, city and county officials have banded together to oppose our right to integration and to attempt to weaken our ADA. Two briefs have been filed arguing the states' right to decide what's best for us. One brief is signed by the Attorneys General of various states. The other by an all-inclusive list of organizations representing states, cities and counties. The *National Conference of State Legislatures*, the *National Governors Association*, the *U.S. Conference of Mayors*, the *National League of Cities* are some of the organizations on that list. They're all agreeing with the *Olmstead* position: the ADA was never "intended to cover institutionalization or in any way affect the pace with which states provide community care." "The state's choice of setting for an individual requiring public care," the *Olmstead's* petition reads, "depends on the individual's mental condition, on the fact and extent of his dangerousness and inability to care for himself, and on fiscal and administrative considerations."

Lucy Gwin, editor of *Mouth* magazine, says: "Here's what I believe. A who's who of vital state and local officials has sent a message not just to the Court but to us. Let's read it for what it is: They can't stand us running around loose. Their bigotry is usually polite, unspoken. Now it's out in the open. Ugly." Lucy is famous for her bluntness. But her observation is the same one that Congress made when the ADA was passed. In *Sec. 2, Findings of Congress*, it is stated that the ADA is necessary because "historically, society has tended to isolate and segregate individuals with disabilities." How can the states now say the ADA allows them to lock us up?

Mobilization of Disabled People

No doubt about it, our community is under attack, and a major mobilization is under way. The alerts have been circulating, handed out at meetings, sent through e-mail and snail mail, posted on webpages and bulletin boards. *Mouth*, "the

Voice of the Disability Nation," has published two special issues dealing entirely with the *Olmstead* threat. ADAPT activists have been hunting down their states' attorneys general, demonstrating and sitting in their offices, demanding they take their names off the amicus brief. And quite a few attorneys general have buckled down under the intense pressure. As of today, 18 out of 26 attorneys general have taken their names off the brief. By the way, NYS Attorney General Eliot Spitzer never signed on.

Our community has also been filing *amici curiae* [friends of the court] briefs. ADAPT, NCIL [National Center for Independent Living] and TASH [ADAPT and TASH are no longer considered acronyms] got together and filed one brief. In it we read: "Public entities have segregated people in institutions because historically that was the way people with disabilities were kept out of sight and away from the public.... [The states] want to reverse what Congress mandated [in the ADA] ... Rather than complying with the ADA and offering services and programs in integrated settings, Petitioners [Olmstead and the state of Georgia] attempt to eviscerate the ADA." Briefs have also been filed by organizations of psychiatric survivors and of mental health consumers, and by self-advocates and people-first organizations (people with mental retardation).

People with different disabilities have different needs and we have in the past all been guilty of putting our needs ahead of others' needs. Some of us with physical disabilities may still hold negative and stereotypical ideas about those of us with mental disabilities, and vice versa. But the threat this case poses to our civil rights has brought us all together. We know that if L.C. and E.W. lose their case, we all lose. No matter what our disability, no matter what label we do or do not carry today, we lose. Even those who don't think they could ever be institutionalized lose, if the ADA's integration mandate gets thrown out the window. This is one decision that will have repercussions in all areas where we now enjoy the ADA's protection. Bob Kafka of ADAPT says: "This decision will affect integration in housing, transportation, employment, you name it."

No doubt about it, we are under attack, and we're realizing we all better stick together. This may be wishful thinking on my part, but I believe we are coming to understand each other and each other's needs a little bit better because of this fight. It's good to see those of us with physical disabilities remembering that we're not just talking about attendant services but about all types of support services; and, remembering, also, the long battle against forced drugging being fought by psychiatric survivors, and therefore insisting that all services be freely chosen and never be forced upon us or be the price to pay for deinstitutionalization. It's good to see excerpts from *Dendron* (the magazine of psychiatric survivors) reprinted in *Mouth*, and *Justice for All* alerts on the *Mad Nation* website. It's good to see the disability rights movement, the psychiatric survivor movement and the self-advocates movement joining forces as never before and organizing for action—as *one* movement, as *one* community.

"Although the initial reaction of mental disability advocates to the court's decision in Olmstead *was ecstatic, the impact of the case in the long run remains to be seen."*

Olmstead Is Unlikely to Lead to Widespread Creation of Community-Based Services for Patients with Mental Illness

Paul S. Appelbaum

Paul S. Appelbaum is a professor of psychiatry at Columbia University. He is a past president of the American Psychiatric Association and the author of many books. In the following viewpoint he comments on the Supreme Court's decision in Olmstead v. L.C., *explaining that although in the past many lower courts had acknowledged the right of psychiatric patients to be treated outside of mental hospitals when this met their needs, the Supreme Court had been reluctant to mandate the creation of community-based treatment facilities. He says there have been lawsuits seeking to establish that such programs are required under the Americans with Disabilities Act;* Olmstead v. L.C. *was one of these suits. After describing the Court's ruling, Appelbaum points out that despite high praise for the decision by advocates for the mentally disabled, it may not improve access to community-based programs because the courts may not compel states to create such programs where they do not already exist.*

Paul S. Appelbaum, "Law & Psychiatry: Least Restrictive Alternative Revisited: Olmstead's Uncertain Mandate for Community-Based Care," *Psychiatric Services*, October 1999. Copyright © 1999 American Psychiatric Association. Reproduced by permission.

More than three decades have passed since the courts first suggested that involuntarily hospitalized psychiatric patients had a right to be treated in the least restrictive alternative setting that met their needs. The doctrine has had its ups and downs since that time; it has been embraced by many lower courts but rejected at the highest appellate level. Now the U.S. Supreme Court has reinvigorated the concept, but has also balanced it with competing concerns, in its important decision in *Olmstead v. L.C.*.

In its heyday in the 1970s, the doctrine of the least restrictive alternative was viewed as a major tool for moving committed patients out of state mental hospitals and into community settings. As supported by a number of decisions in lower federal courts, the doctrine rested on the argument that the state could not deprive persons of liberty to an extent unwarranted to meet its legitimate goals. Thus although the state may have had the power to commit persons with mental illness to inpatient treatment against their will to protect those persons or others, it could not do so when means less restrictive of liberty were available to accomplish the same ends. In short, if patients could be safely treated in the community, there was no warrant for their confinement in inpatient settings.

The application of this reasoning about the least restrictive alternative appeared straightforward, so long as community-based facilities existed to which patients could be transferred. What happened, however, if a state had failed to create enough such placements? Could the courts compel states to redirect funds away from state hospitals and into community care? Although the enthusiastic lower-court judges who undertook to reform state mental health systems in the activist 1970s believed the answer was yes, and ordered states to act accordingly, the U.S. Supreme Court took a somewhat different view.

Two decisions of the high court underscored the justices' reluctance to have courts involved in mandating the creation of community treatment facilities, thereby altering states' spending priorities, a quintessential legislative function. The court first refused to read apparently clear statutory language in the 1975 federal Developmentally Disabled Assistance and Bill of Rights Act as creating a right to treatment in the community, holding that the language was merely "hortatory". Then, in its 1982 decision in *Youngberg v. Romeo*, the court pulled the rug out from under a constitutional right to treatment in the least restrictive alternative altogether. Although the concept had already made its way into a number of state commitment statutes, the federal courts seemed to be out of the business of compelling states to create alternative treatment venues in the community.

Impact of the ADA

Recently attempts have been made to breathe new life into the idea of a federally enforceable right to the least restrictive alternative by means of the Americans With Disabilities Act (ADA). Passed in 1990, the ADA takes a multipronged approach to promoting the integration of persons with disabilities into the social and economic life of the U.S. Among its provisions is Title II, which covers public services provided by governmental entities. Section 12132 orders that "no qualified individual with a disability shall, by reason of such disability, be excluded from participation in or be denied the benefits of the services, programs, or activities of a public entity, or be subjected to discrimination by any such entity."

The Attorney General was ordered by Congress to promulgate regulations to implement this section, coordinating them with similar regulations governing the Rehabilitation Act of 1973. One of the resulting regulations reads as follows: "A public entity shall administer services, programs, and activities *in the most integrated setting appropriate to the needs of qualified individuals with disabilities*" (emphasis added). A second regulation requires that public entities make reasonable modifications to their program to avoid discrimination on the basis of disability, "unless the public entity can demonstrate that making the modifications would *fundamentally alter* the nature of the service, program, or activity" (emphasis added).

Opponents of unnecessary hospitalization of persons with mental illness and mental retardation saw in the Attorney General's regulations an opportunity to use the ADA to force states to treat patients in the most integrated settings possible. A number of law suits were filed in the lower federal courts asking that states transfer patients to community-based care, with some considerable success. Inevitably, however, the states resisted these efforts to impose new mandates on their mental health systems, making eventual review by the U.S. Supreme Court all but inevitable.

The case that brought the issue to the nation's highest court was filed on behalf of two Georgia women with mental retardation and comorbid psychiatric disorders, known by their initials, L.C. and E.W. After being admitted voluntarily to Georgia Regional Hospital in Atlanta in May 1992, L.C.'s schizophrenia was treated and stabilized. By May 1993 her treatment team agreed that she did not require further hospitalization but could have her needs met in a state-supported community facility. Placement in that facility, however, took nearly three more years.

E.W.'s story was similar. She was voluntarily hospitalized in February 1995 with a diagnosis of personality disorder. A month later the state sought to discharge her to a homeless shelter, a plan aborted when her attorney filed a complaint. By 1996 E.W.'s therapist concluded that she could be treated in a community setting, but she was not discharged until several months after the district court's decision in the legal action that had been brought in the meantime.

Filing suit in federal district court, L.C. maintained, among other things, that the state's failure to place her in a community facility after her treaters deemed it appropriate violated

Title II of the ADA. E.W. intervened in the case with a similar claim. The district court found in favor of the plaintiffs, rejecting the state's defense that inadequate funding, not discrimination, had led to the failure to place these women in community-based facilities. Nor was it persuaded by the state's claim that ordering the placement of these patients would fundamentally alter the state's mental health services in such a way that it should be exempt from the requirements of the ADA. Existing state programs, after all, provided community services for just such persons.

When the state of Georgia appealed to the Eleventh Circuit Court of Appeals, that court upheld the district court's finding, but ordered additional hearings on whether the court's order to provide community care to these two plaintiffs would require a fundamental alteration in Georgia's mental health services. Georgia again appealed, this time to the U.S. Supreme Court.

The Supreme Court Ruling

Writing for the majority, Justice Ruth Bader Ginsburg upheld the lower courts' finding that "unjustified institutional isolation of persons with disabilities is a form of discrimination" that was forbidden by the ADA. She noted that institutional placement both "perpetuates unwarranted assumptions that persons so isolated are incapable or unworthy of participating in community life," and "severely diminishes the everyday life activities of individuals, including family relations, social contacts, work options, economic independence, educational advancement, and cultural enrichment." Persons with mental disabilities are discriminated against because they must forgo community life to receive the medical treatment they need, whereas persons without mental disabilities can receive medical services without sacrificing their ties to the community.

Having acknowledged that disabled persons with mental disabilities could look to the ADA to define a right to community-based care, Justice [Ruth Bader] Ginsburg, with the support of a plurality of only four justices, attempted to define the limits of that right. Existing regulations make clear that remedies that would "fundamentally alter" the services provided by the state are not required by the ADA. Justice Ginsburg took issue with the approach of the lower courts to this matter.

She wrote, "If the expense entailed in placing one or two people in a community-based treatment program is properly measured for reasonableness against the State's entire mental health budget, it is unlikely that a State, relying on the fundamental-alteration defense, could ever prevail." Rather, she held that Georgia should be allowed to show on remand that, "in the allocation of available resources, immediate relief for the plaintiffs would be inequitable, given the responsibility the State has undertaken for the care and treatment of a large and diverse population of persons with mental disabilities."

The Supreme Court's caution in not wanting to override state decisions about allocation of resources was evident in other ways as well. Justice Ginsburg stressed that a state with a reasonable program of community care, with "a waiting list that moved at a reasonable pace not controlled by the State's endeavors to keep its institutions fully populated," fulfilled the ADA requirements. Moreover, states could usually rely on the judgments of their own professionals in determining whether community-based care was appropriate.

In an opinion concurring in the judgment, Justice Anthony Kennedy said explicitly that "a State may not be forced to create a community-treatment program where none exists," although the majority's position on this question is far from clear. He reviewed the unhappy consequences of willy-nilly deinstitutionalization, underscoring the point that forcing people out of institutions who truly needed to be there was not the court's intent.

Although the initial reaction of mental disability advocates to the court's decision in *Olmstead* was ecstatic, the impact of the case in the long run remains to be seen. It may lead to greater equity for persons confined in state facilities—even if they are there voluntarily—with regard to access to existing community resources. But it is unclear to what extent the U.S. Supreme Court will support lower courts in compelling states to create community alternatives that do not now exist. No bright line has been identified to separate states that can rely on the fundamental-alteration defense from those that cannot. The reluctance of the courts to trample on executive branch prerogatives has always been the bugaboo of the least restrictive alternative doctrine. Whatever else it may accomplish, the decision in *Olmstead v. L.C.* is unlikely to precipitate the widespread creation of community-based services for persons with mental disabilities.

"Unnecessary institutionalization of people is the most egregious of the many wrongs endured by our clients with mental disabilities."

Olmstead Was a Victory for People Who Have No Voice

Atlanta Legal Aid Society

The Atlanta Legal Aid Society is a nonprofit organization that provides referrals and legal representation to people who otherwise cannot obtain access to the court system—the poor, minorities, the elderly, those disabled by mental illness or long-term diseases, and recent immigrants. Its attorneys represented the plaintiffs in Olmstead v. L.C. and E.W., *in which the Supreme Court decided that except where the cost is prohibitive, mentally disabled people whose doctors say they do not need institutionalization must be released to community-based care programs. The following viewpoint summarizes the case and presents the reactions of the lead attorney and officers of the Legal Aid Society who attended the Supreme Court oral arguments. It also includes an update on what happened to the plaintiffs later in their lives.*

T his case of first impression in the Eleventh Circuit sought community residential placements for L.C. and E.W., who had spent the majority of their lives in mental institutions. For several years, their treatment teams acknowledged that they no longer met the requirements for involuntary confine-

Atlanta Legal Aid Society, "Olmstead v. LC and EW: Landmark Case," October 15, 2007. Copyright © 2007 Atlanta Legal Aid Society, Inc. All Rights Reserved. Reproduced by permission. www.atlantalegalaid.org/impact.htm.

ment, but refused to release them to a community-based program with appropriate services. The case, filed in 1995, presents a claim under the Americans With Disabilities Act. Our position is that the State of Georgia can no longer provide disability services to a mentally or physically disabled person in an institutional setting if he or she could be served in a more integrated, community-based setting. The State appealed a favorable decision of the federal District Court granting summary judgment for our plaintiffs. Oral argument before the Eleventh Circuit Court of Appeals was in November 1997. The Eleventh Circuit ruled that the State's failure to provide integrated community services under these circumstances violated the Americans with Disabilities Act.

The State appealed to the United States Supreme Court to reverse that ruling. Now known as *Olmstead v. L.C. and E.W.*, it was heard on April 21, 1999. This is the first U.S. Supreme Court case involving the "integration mandate" of the Americans With Disabilities Act. Although both plaintiffs were receiving community services in response to the lawsuit, the case continued because the State of Georgia had not changed its policies, and the situation could have arisen again.

After L.C. and E.W. moved from institutional life into the community, each progressed in ways that reveal the monotony of their former circumstances—for example, L.C. likes long neighborhood walks and has (after many years) reconnected with her mom and sister. She visits the mall and picks out her own clothes. She has favorite meals and has learned to plan a menu. She quit a 3-pack a day cigarette habit. She speaks clearly and communicates well. She has two close friends at the group home. She loved her first airplane trip to Washington, and her meeting with a variety of media in connection with the Supreme Court consideration of her case.

E.W. spent a year in a group home, where she decorated her own room, organized picture albums, and made regular weekend trips home to be with her extended family. She lived in a house with a caretaker and friend, who worked during the day while E.W. was at her pre-vocational program. E.W. became increasingly independent, taking complete responsibility for her own medical needs, an area that institutional doctors felt was problematic. [She] was able to shop, cook, choose her own clothes, and attend family events and celebrations.

Several Legal Aid lawyers, the Board's President and Vice President attended the argument. Most used words such as "awe-inspiring" and "re-energizing" to describe the experience.

Comment of Sue Jamieson, Attorney for L.C. and E.W.

"The two legal aid clients who were Plaintiffs in this case were, like each of our clients, people with little income and, by conventional standards, undervalued. We represented them simply because they called our office—exactly why we represent all of our clients. The fact that we filed a case in federal court raising an ADA claim is mostly because unnecessary institutionalization of people is the most egregious of the many wrongs endured by our clients with mental disabilities—like spousal abuse, illegal evictions, consumer fraud, etc., etc., etc. . . . The case began like all our cases with the everyday effort to represent someone who called the office.

"The question these clients asked was, in essence, 'Can you help me out of this outrageous situation?' The question we are asked every day over and over and over.

"How the question ended up in the Supreme Court is as random as the lottery. Fewer than 100 of 7000 petitions for certiorari are granted each year. . . . Somehow, one of those many questions got blown up to an exaggerated size, just one of our many questions that we all persist in asking daily in our work, hoping to shift the balance slightly.

"What a great feeling it was to be annoying the Supreme Court with one of our clients' questions!

"Thank you for so much good will, good wishes and support."

Comment of Judge Patsy Y. Porter, 1999 ALAS President

"I was both proud and humbled to be there. We have an awesome responsibility. The things we do affect everyone's lives. Win, lose or draw, I still think we win because we stand up for the rights of people who would not otherwise have a voice. That in itself is why we have Legal Aid. We are protecting the Constitutional rights of everyone in this country. And no matter what happens now, we have done the right thing for these clients."

The Death of a Hero

Ms. Elaine Wilson, 53, died on December 5, 2004. She was a plaintiff in the case *L.C. and E.W. v. Olmstead....*

After filing the case, Ms. Wilson was provided with community services and she lived in a home with a friend and care-provider. Although she had been institutionalized more than 30 times prior to bringing the lawsuit, once she was provided with alternative community-based options, she enjoyed an active life in the community. She developed her own advocacy skills, speaking and presenting in Georgia and in other places in the country about her own experiences and her hopes for the freedom of other institutionalized persons. She was known and loved by many in the disability community who were inspired by her determination and interest in reaching out to others once she finally secured her own freedom.

Final Settlement

On July 11, 2000, in the courtroom of Judge Marvin Shoob, the *L.C. and E.W. v. Olmstead* case came to a formal close with the signing of the final settlement agreement.

Sue Jamieson, lead counsel for Legal Aid's clients, began with a presentation crediting the lawyers that have been involved, the courage of the clients, and the judicial pioneering of Judge Shoob for this milestone. Sue described the long litigation road, and the benefits of the settlement to the clients.

The court then called on the *guardian ad litem*, Jonathan Zimring, who had high praise for the legal team that represented his clients.

Perhaps the most moving statements came from the clients themselves, who were invited to address the court. Lois said that now that the case was over, she hoped it would help other people. Elaine said that now she feels loved and cared for where she lives. In the institution, she had felt like she was sitting in a little box with no way out. They both spoke of little things, such as making Kool Aid and being outdoors, that meant so much to them.

Judge Shoob then called on Steve Gottlieb, Executive Director of Atlanta Legal Aid, who mentioned that the case had been portrayed as the *Brown v. Board of Education* of disability law, and as a defining moment in the Americans With Disabilities Act.

Judge Shoob then declared that the settlement agreement was approved and was now in effect. He complimented Sue Jamieson, David Webster, and others for what he described as an outstanding effort and a splendid result.

Lois Curtis: Folk artist

Lois Curtis, one of the original *Olmstead* plaintiffs, has been busy since being freed from a lifetime of repeated institutionalizations. She enjoys living in her own home, with the aid of community based services; she has reconnected with her family, and she has made new friends.

Her own experiences with institutionalization, and the Supreme Court case that freed her, have prompted a passion for advocacy. "I want to tell everybody, so people can get out." The Tubman African American Museum recognized Lois with the "Act of Courage Award" for "standing up and taking action during challenging circumstances to make a difference for yourself and the lives of others."

Lois has also found success as a folk artist, and has had several well received shows at several galleries, including Arts for All Gallery in the Healy Building in downtown Atlanta, the Temple Gallery in Decatur, and other galleries throughout the U.S.

Organizations to Contact

The editors have compiled the following list of organizations concerned with the issues debated in this book. The descriptions are derived from materials provided by the organizations. All have publications or information available for interested readers. The list was compiled on the date of publication of the present volume; the information provided here may change. Be aware that many organizations take several weeks or longer to respond to inquiries, so allow as much time as possible.

Bazelon Center for Mental Health Law
1101 Fifteenth Street NW, Suite 1212, Washington, DC   20005
(202) 467-5730 • fax: 202-223-0409
e-mail: info@bazelong.org
Web site: www.bazelon.org

Bazelon Center attorneys provide technical support on mental health law issues and co-counsel selected lawsuits. The Center's mission is to protect and advance the rights of adults and children who have mental disabilities, believing that they should exercise their own life choices and have access to the resources that enable them to participate fully in their communities. Its Web site contains news, information about specific cases, and downloadable publications.

Children and Adults Against Drugging America (CHAADA)
e-mail: info@chaada.org
Web site: www.chaada.org

CHAADA is a member-based organization that aims to "raise awareness about the overmedicating of America and the deception occurring within the psychiatric profession, the inhumanity of involuntary hospitalization, the preying on innocent people, especially children, in order to turn a profit, and the dangers of the drugs used to treat alleged mental illnesses." It believes in natural healing and alternative treatments. Its Web site contains extensive informational material.

International Center for the Study of Psychiatry and Psychology (ICSPP)

2808 Kohler Memorial Drive, Suite 1, Sheboygan, WI 53081
Web site: http://icspp.org

ICSPP is a research and educational network devoted to educating professionals and the public concerning the impact of mental health theories on public policy and the effects of therapeutic practices upon individual well-being, personal freedom, and family and community values. It was founded by Peter Breggin, a psychiatrist well known for his opposition to the use of drugs and especially to their forcible administration. The ICSPP Web site contains articles critical of psychiatric drugs.

Law Project for Psychiatric Rights (PsychRights)

406 G Street, Suite 206, Anchorage, AK 99501
Web Site: http://psychrights.org

PsychRights is a nonprofit, tax-exempt public-interest law firm whose mission is to mount a strategic legal campaign against forced psychiatric drugging and electroshock in the United States. Its Web site has a vast amount of up-to-date information on legal aspects of psychiatric treatment, news, and personal stories of harm done by psychiatric drugs, plus many videos.

Mental Health America

2000 N. Beauregard Street, 6th Floor, Alexandria, VA 22311
(800) 969-6642 • fax: (703) 684-5968
Web site: www.mentalhealthamerica.net

Mental Health America (formerly the National Mental Health Association) is the country's leading nonprofit dedicated to helping all people live mentally healthier lives. With more than 320 affiliates nationwide, it represents a growing movement of Americans who promote mental wellness for the health and well-being of the nation. It is opposed to involuntary treatment and believes that persons with mental illness have a right to make their own decisions about their care. Its Web site contains many detailed position statements as well as information about specific conditions, services available, and legislative advocacy.

MindFreedom International (MFI)

P.O. Box 11284, Eugene, OR   97440-3484
(877) 623-7743 • fax: (541) 345-3737
e-mail: office@mindfreedom.org
Web site: http://mindfreedom.org

MFI is an independent nonprofit coalition of former psychiatric patients and their supporters that defends human rights and promotes humane alternatives for mental and emotional well-being. Its Web site contains information and news about the damage done by psychiatric drugs and the abuse of patients confined in psychiatric institutions.

National Alliance on Mental Illness (NAMI)

2107 Wilson Blvd., Suite 300, Arlington, VA   22201-3042
(703) 524-7600 • fax: (703) 524-9094
Web Site: www.nami.org

NAMI is a large grassroots mental health advocacy organization with many state and local affiliates. Its support and public education efforts are focused on educating Americans about mental illness, offering resources to those in need, and insisting that mental illness become a high national priority. It supports treatment with psychiatric drugs. Its Web site contains information about mental illness, its treatment, and services available that are compatible with the organization's views.

National Association for Rights Protection and Advocacy (NARPA)

P.O. Box 40585, Tuscaloosa, AL   35404
(205) 464-0101
e-mail: narpa@aol.com
Web site: www.narpa.org

NARPA is dedicated to promoting policies and pursuing those strategies that represent the preferred options of people who have been labeled mentally disabled. It is committed to advocating the abolishing of all forced treatment laws. It believes that the recipients of mental health services are capable of and entitled to make their own choices and are, above all, equal citizens under the law. Its Web site contains many links to news and relevant articles in the media and to other organizations.

National Council on Disability

1331 F Street NW, Suite 850, Washington, DC   20004
(202) 272-2004 • fax (202) 272-2022
Web site: www.ncd.gov

NCD is an independent federal agency that provides advice to the president, Congress, and executive branch agencies to promote policies, programs, practices, and procedures that guarantee equal opportunity for all individuals with disabilities. Its Web site contains a number of papers involving the treatment of people with mental illness, including the important report "From Privileges to Rights: People Labeled with Psychiatric Disabilities Speak for Themselves."

National Institute of Mental Health (NIMH)

6001 Executive Blvd., Room 8184, MSC 9663
Bethesda, MD   20892-9663
(866) 615-6464 • fax: (301) 443-4279
e-mail: nimhinfo@nih.gov
Web site: www.nimh.nih.gov

NIMH is part of the National Institutes of Health (NIH), a component of the U.S. Department of Health and Human Services. Its mission is to transform the understanding and treatment of mental illnesses through basic and clinical research, paving the way for prevention, recovery and cure. Its Web site contains news, statistics, and information about its research.

Treatment Advocacy Center

200 N. Glebe Road, Suite 730, Arlington, VA   22203
(703) 294-6001 • fax: (703) 294-6010
Web site: www.treatmentadvocacycenter.org

The Treatment Advocacy Center is a national nonprofit organization dedicated to eliminating barriers to the timely and effective treatment of severe mental illnesses. It promotes laws, policies, and practices for the delivery of psychiatric care and supports the development of innovative treatments for and research into the causes of severe and persistent psychiatric illnesses. It believes that too many people with mental illness are untreated and advocates court-ordered treatment (including medication) for individuals who have a history of medication noncompliance.

World Network of Users and Survivors of Psychiatry (WNUSP)

Store Glasvej 49, Odense C   5000
  Denmark
e-mail: admin@wnusp.net
Web site: http://wnusp.rafus.dk

WNUSP, an international organization of present and past recipients of mental health services, is dedicated to protecting the human rights, self-determination, and dignity of all users/ survivors throughout the world. Its Web site contains a position paper listing in detail the rights to which it believes persons with mental illness are entitled, plus links to reports of a United Nations commission and other organizations that oppose coerced psychiatric treatment.

For Further Research

Books

Peter Bartlett and Ralph Sandland, *Mental Health Law: Policy and Practice*. New York: Oxford University Press, 2007.

Peter R. Breggin, *Toxic Psychiatry*. New York: St. Martin's, 1994.

Michael G. Brock, Samuel Saks, and Ralph Slovenko, *Contemporary Issues in Family Law and Mental Health*. Springfield, IL: Charles C. Thomas, 2008.

Enoch Callaway, *Asylum: A Mid-Century Madhouse and Its Lessons About Our Mentally Ill Today*. Westport, CT: Praeger, 2007.

Charles Patrick Ewing and Joseph T. McCann, *Minds on Trial: Great Cases in Law and Psychology*. New York: Oxford University Press, 2006.

Judith Lynn Failer, *Who Qualifies for Rights: Homelessness, Mental Illness, and Civil Commitment*. Ithaca, NY: Cornell University Press, 2002.

Richard G. Frank and Sherry A. Glied, *Better But Not Well: Mental Health Policy in the United States since 1950*. Baltimore: Johns Hopkins University Press, 2006.

Lynda E. Frost and Richard J. Bonnie, eds., *The Evolution of Mental Health Law*. Washington, DC: American Psychological Association, 2001.

Gerald N. Grob and Howard H. Goldman, *The Dilemma of Federal Mental Health Policy: Radical Reform or Incremental Change?* New Brunswick, NJ: Rutgers University Press, 2006.

Bryan Hilliard, *The U.S. Supreme Court and Medical Ethics: From Contraception to Managed Health Care*. St. Paul, MN: Paragon House, 2004.

Rael Jean Isaac and Virginia C. Armat, *Madness in the Streets: How Psychiatry and the Law Abandoned the Mentally Ill*. Arlington, VA: Treatment Advocacy Center, 2000.

Robert G. Meyer and Christopher M. Weaver, *Law and Mental Health: A Case-Based Approach*. New York: Guilford Press, 2005.

Mary Beth Pfeiffer, *Crazy in America: The Hidden Tragedy of Our Criminalized Mentally Ill*. New York: Carroll & Graf, 2007.

Elyn R. Saks, *Refusing Care: Forced Treatment and the Rights of the Mentally Ill*. Chicago: University of Chicago Press, 2002.

Christopher Slobogin, *Minding Justice: Laws that Deprive People with Mental Disability of Life and Liberty*. Cambridge, MA: Harvard University Press, 2006.

Susan Stefan, *Unequal Rights: Discrimination Against People with Mental Disabilities and the Americans with Disabilities Act*. Washington, DC: American Psychological Association, 2001.

Thomas Szasz, *Coercion as Cure: A Critical History of Psychiatry*. New Brunswick, NJ: Transaction Publishers, 2007.

Graham Thornicroft, *Shunned: Discrimination Against People with Mental Illness*. New York: Oxford University Press, 2006.

Carol A.B. Warren, *The Court of Last Resort: Mental Illness and the Law*. Chicago: University of Chicago Press, 1982.

Robert Whitaker, *Mad in America: Bad Science, Bad Medicine, and the Enduring Mistreatment of the Mentally Ill.* Cambridge, MA: Perseus, 2003.

Rogers H. Wright and Nicholas A. Cummings, eds., *Destructive Trends in Mental Health: The Well-Intentioned Path to Harm.* New York: Routledge, 2005.

Periodicals

Rudolph Alexander Jr., "The Right to Treatment in Mental and Correctional Institutions," *Social Work*, March 1989.

George J. Annas, "Forcible Medication for Courtroom Competence: The Case of Charles Sell," *New England Journal of Medicine*, May 27, 2004.

Paul S. Appelbaum, "Can Mental Patients Say No to Drugs?" *New York Times*, March 21, 1982.

"Bazelon Center Report Chronicles Unfulfilled Promise of Olmstead Decision," *Mental Health Weekly*, June 29, 2009.

Nina Bernstein, "Freed Inmates Must Get Care if Mentally Ill," *New York Times*, July 13, 2000.

———, "Treatment Plan Is Sought After Inmates Are Freed," *New York Times*, August 25, 1999.

Ralph Blumenthal, "A Growing Plea for Mercy for the Mentally Ill on Death Row," *New York Times*, November 23, 2006.

Angel Castillo, "Mental Patients' Right to Refuse Medication Is Contested in Jersey," *New York Times*, March 28, 1981.

Ellen Wright Clayton, "From *Rogers* to *Rivers*: The Rights of the Mentally Ill to Refuse Medication," *American Journal of Law and Medicine*, vol. 13, no.1, 1987.

"Defining 'Disability' Down," *New York Times*, April 20, 1999.

James R. Eisenberg, "Forcibly Medicating Death Row Inmates with Mental Illness—An Ethical Dilemma," *Behavioral Health Management*, January 1, 2004.

Daphne Eviatar, "If Sanity Is Forced on a Defendant, Who Is on Trial?" *New York Times*, June 21, 2003.

Gabrielle Glaser, "'Mad Pride' Fights a Stigma," *New York Times*, May 11, 2008.

Daniel Goleman, "Lawsuits Try to Force Care for the Mentally Ill," *New York Times*, April 24, 1984.

Linda Greenhouse, "Forcing Psychiatric Drugs On Defendants Is Weighed," *New York Times*, March 4, 2003.

———, "Justices Restrict a 'Bill of Rights' for the Retarded," *New York Times*, April 21, 1981

———, "States Limited on Institutionalization," *New York Times*, June 23, 1999.

Bernard E. Harcourt, "The Mentally Ill, Behind Bars," *New York Times*, January 15, 2007.

Robin Herman, "Shelters for Mental Patients Sought in Suit Against State," *New York Times*, August 11, 1982.

Sarah C. Kellogg, "The Due Process Right to a Safe and Humane Environment for Patients in State Custody: The Voluntary/Involuntary Distinction," *American Journal of Law and Medicine*, vol. 23, no. 2, 1997.

Barry Latzer, "Between Madness and Death: The Medicate-to-Execute Controversy," *Criminal Justice Ethics*, Summer/Fall 2003.

Michael Levin-Epstein, "Should the Courts Be Involved? Experts Debate Whether 'Forced' Outpatient Treatment Makes Sense," *Behavioral Healthcare*, June 1, 2006.

Clifford J. Levy, "For Mentally Ill, Death and Misery," *New York Times*, April 28, 2002.

————, "Suit Says State Is Segregating Mentally Ill," *New York Times*, July 1, 2003.

Loren Mosher et al., "Are Psychiatrists Betraying Their Patients?" *Psychology Today*, October 1, 1999.

Robert Pear, "U.S. Seeks More Care for Disabled Outside Institutions," *New York Times*, February 13, 2000.

Jeffrey L. Poston, "How Olmstead Impacts State Mental Health Policy," *Behavioral Health Management*, May 1, 2004.

Alissa Quart, "Listening to Madness," *Newsweek*, May 18, 2009.

Warren Richey, "Crucial Case for Mentally Disabled," *Christian Science Monitor*, April 21, 1999.

Sara Rosenbaum, "The Olmstead Decision: Implications for State Health Policy," *Health Affairs*, September/October 2000.

Michael J. Stoil, "The Last Hurrah for State Hospitals?" *Behavioral Health Management*, March 1, 1999.

Joel Teitelbaum, Taylor Burke, and Sara Rosenbaum, "*Olmstead v. L.C.* and the Americans with Disabilities Act: Implications for Public Health Policy and Practice," *Public Health Reports*, May/June 2004.

Hal Wortzel, "The Right to Refuse Treatment," *Psychiatric Times*, December 1, 2006.

Athar Yawar, "The Fool on the Hill," *Lancet*, February 21, 2009.

Index